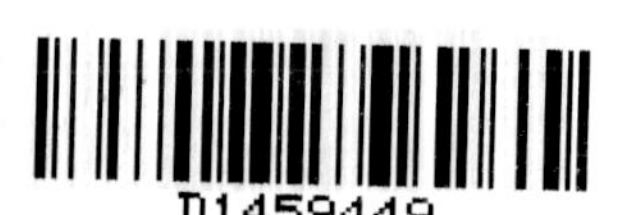

Teach® urself

Traveller's FRENCH

Teach Yourself®

Traveller's FRENCH

By bestselling author *Elisabeth Smith*

First published in Great Britain in 1998 as Teach Yourself Instant French by Hodder Education, an Hachette UK company.

First published in US in 1998 as Teach Yourself Instant French by The McGraw-Hill Companies, Inc.

This edition published 2013.

British Library Cataloguing in Publication Data: a catalogue record for this title is available from the British Library.

Library of Congress Catalog Card Number: on file.

10 9 8 7 6 5 4 3 2 1

Typeset by Cenveo® Publisher Services.

Printed and bound by CPI Group (UK) Ltd, Croydon, CR0 4YY.

Hodder & Stoughton policy is to use papers that are natural, renewable and recyclable products and made from wood grown in sustainable forests. The logging and manufacturing processes are expected to conform to the environmental regulations of the country of origin.

Hodder & Stoughton Ltd

338 Euston Road

London NW1 3BH

www.hodder.co.uk

Contents

Read this first

If, like me, you usually skip introductions, don't. Read on. You need to know how **Traveller's French** works and why. You'll want to know how you are going to speak French in just six weeks.

When I decided to write this series I first called it *Barebones*, because that's what you want: *no frills*, *no fuss*, *just the bare bones and go*. So in **Traveller's French** you'll find:

- Only 389 words to say, well ... nearly everything.
- No tricky grammar – just some useful tips.
- No time wasters such as *the pen of my aunt*...
- No phrasebook phrases for bunjee jumping from the Eiffel Tower.
- No need to be perfect. Mistakes won't spoil your success.

I've put some 30 years of teaching experience into this course. I know how people learn. I also know how long they are motivated by a new project before the boredom sets in (a few weeks). And I am well aware how little time they can spare to study each day (about ½ hour). That's why you'll complete **Traveller's French** in six weeks and get away with 35 minutes a day.

Of course there is some learning to do, but I have tried to make it as much fun as possible. You'll meet Tom and Kate Walker on holiday in France. They do the kind of things you need to know about: shopping, eating out and getting about. They chat to the locals, ask a lot of questions and even understand the answers ... most of the time. As you will note, Tom and Kate speak French all the time, even to each other. What paragons of virtue.

To get the most out of this course, there are only three things you really should do:

- Follow the Day-by-day guide as suggested. Please don't skip bits and short-change your success. Everything is there for a reason.
- If you are a complete beginner and have only bought the book, treat yourself to the recording as well. It will help you to speak faster and with confidence.
- Don't skip the next page (**How this book works**). It's essential for your success.

When you have filled in your Certificate at the end of the book and can speak **Traveller's French**, I would like to hear from you. Why not visit my website www.elisabeth-smith.co.uk, e-mail me at elisabeth.smith@hodder.co.uk, or write to me care of Hodder Education, 338 Euston Road, London, NW1 3BH?

And please join me on:

Facebook at www.facebook.com/elisabethsmithlanguages

Twitter at www.twitter.com/LanguagesESmith

Elisabeth Smith

How this book works

Traveller's French has been structured for your rapid success. This is how it works:

Day-by-day guide Stick to it. If you miss a day, add one.

Dialogues Follow Tom and Kate through France.

The English of Weeks 1–3 is in 'French-speak' to get you tuned in. 'French-speak' is English imitating the expressions of French, for example, *We can it take at 7 o'clock*. You'll soon get a feel for the language.

New words Don't fight them, don't skip them – learn them! The **Flash cards** and the recording will help you. Get your friends or family to test you. Or take the **Flash cards** with you when you are out and about.

Good news grammar After you read it you can forget half and still succeed. That's why it's good news.

Flash words and flash sentences Read about these building blocks in the **Flash card** section. Then use them! They'll reduce learning time by 50%.

Learn by heart Obligatory! Memorizing puts you on the fast track to speaking in full sentences. When you know all six pieces you'll be able to speak in French for six minutes without drawing breath.

Let's speak French You will be doing the talking – in French.

Let's speak more French – fast and fluently Optional extras for more speaking practice without pausing and stumbling.

Spot the keys Listen to rapid French and make sense of it. Find the key words among a seemingly unintelligible string of sentences and get the gist of what's being said – an essential skill.

Say it simply Learn how to use simple French to say what you want to say. Don't be shy.

Test your progress Mark your own test and be amazed by the result.

Answers This is where you'll find the answers to the exercises.

🔊 This icon asks you to switch on the recording.

Pronunciation If you don't know about it and don't have the recording go straight to Week 1 **Pronunciation**. You need to know about pronunciation before you can start Week 1.

Progress chart Enter your score each week and monitor your progress. Are you going for very good or outstanding?

Dictionary Forgotten one of the new words? Look it up in the dictionary.

Certificate It's on the last page. In six weeks it will have your name on it.

Progress chart

At the end of each week record your test score on the progress chart below.

At the end of the course throw out your worst result – anybody can have a bad week – and add up your five best weekly scores. Divide the total by five to get your average score and overall course result. Write your result – outstanding, excellent, very good or good – on your **Certificate** at the end of the book.

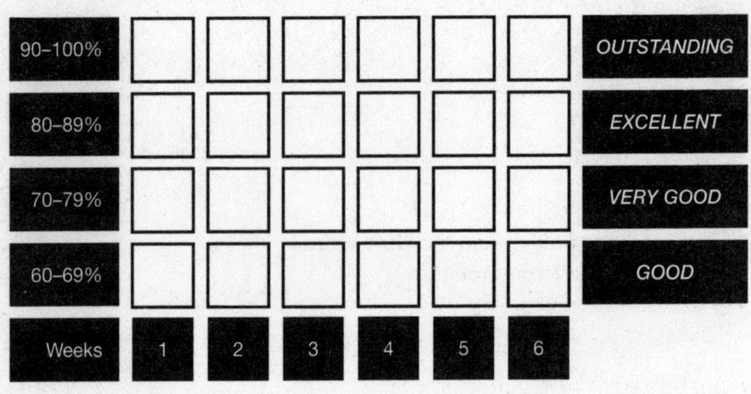

Total of five best weeks =

divided by five =

Your final result _____%

Week 1

Day-by-day guide

Invest 35 minutes a day – or a little more if you can.

Day zero

- Open the book and read **Read this first.**
- Now read **How this book works.**

Day one

- Read **In the aeroplane.**
- Listen to/Read **Dans l'avion.**
- Listen to/Read the **New words,** then learn some of them.

Day two

- Repeat **Dans l'avion** and the **New words.**
- Listen to/Read **Pronunciation.**
- Learn more **New words.**
- Use the **Flash words** to help you.

Day three

- Learn all the **New words** until you know them well.
- Read and learn the **Good news grammar**.

Day four

- Cut out and learn the ten **Flash sentences.**
- Listen to/Read **Learn by heart**.

Day five

- Listen to/Read **Let's speak French.**
- Revise! Tomorrow you'll be testing your progress.

Day six

- Listen to/Read **Let's speak more French** (optional).
- Listen to/Read **Let's speak French – fast and fluently** (optional).
- Translate **Test your progress.**

Day seven is your day off!

In the aeroplane

Tom and Kate Walker are off to France. They board flight QS 16 to Marseille via Paris and squeeze past fellow passenger Henri.

Tom Excuse me, we have the seats 9a and 9b.

Henri Ah, yes, one moment, please.

Tom Hello. We are Tom and Kate Walker.

Henri Good day. My name is Cardin.

Tom Pierre Cardin?

Henri No, unfortunately. I am Henri Cardin.

Tom We are going to Marseille. You too?

Henri No, I am going to Paris but I am from Toulouse.

Tom I was in Toulouse in May. It is a beautiful town. I was in Toulouse for the work.

Henri What do you do?

Tom I work with computers.

Henri And you, Mrs Walker? What do you do?

Kate I was at Mobil. Now I work at Rover. It is better.

Henri Are you from London?

Kate No, we are from Manchester. We were one year in New York and three years in London. We are now in Birmingham.

Henri I was at Renault. Now I work for the Bank of France.

Tom Have you a good job at the bank?

Henri The work is not interesting but well paid. I need a lot of money. I have a big house, a Mercedes and four children. My wife is American. She has her parents in Los Angeles and a girlfriend in Dallas, and she is always on the telephone. It costs a lot.

Kate We are on holiday. You too?

Henri No, unfortunately. My holidays are in September. We are going to Provence but without the children. We have a house in St Tropez without telephone – and we go to St Tropez without mobile!

Dans l'avion

🔊 CD1, tr 2

Tom and Kate Walker are off to France. They board flight QS 16 to Marseille via Paris and squeeze past fellow passenger Henri.

Tom Excusez-moi, nous avons les places neuf a et neuf b.

Henri Ah oui, un moment, s'il vous plaît.

Tom Bonjour. Nous sommes Tom et Kate Walker.

Henri Bonjour. Mon nom est Cardin.

Tom Pierre Cardin?

Henri Non, malheureusement. Je suis Henri Cardin.

Tom Nous allons à Marseille. Vous aussi?

Henri Non, je vais à Paris mais je suis de Toulouse.

Tom J'étais à Toulouse en mai. C'est une belle ville. J'étais à Toulouse pour le travail.

Henri Que faites-vous?

Tom Je travaille avec des ordinateurs.

Henri Et vous, Madame Walker? Que faites-vous?

Kate J'étais chez Mobil. Actuellement, je travaille chez Rover. C'est mieux.

Henri Vous êtes de Londres?

Kate Non, nous sommes de Manchester. Nous étions un an à New York et trois ans à Londres. Nous sommes actuellement à Birmingham.

Henri J'étais chez Renault. Actuellement je travaille pour la Banque de France.

Tom Avez-vous un bon poste à la banque?

Henri Le travail n'est pas intéressant mais bien payé. J'ai besoin de beaucoup d'argent. J'ai une grande maison, une Mercédès et quatre enfants. Ma femme est américaine. Elle a ses parents à Los Angeles et une amie à Dallas, et elle est toujours au téléphone. Ça coûte très cher.

Kate Nous sommes en vacances. Vous aussi?

Henri Non, malheureusement. Mes vacances sont en septembre. Nous allons en Provence mais sans les enfants. Nous avons une maison à St Tropez sans téléphone – et nous allons à St Tropez sans portable!

New words

🔊 CD1, tr 3

Learn your vocabulary by covering up the French words. Then go down the list of the English words and see how many you can remember. Always say the French words out loud.

dans in, inside
le, la, l', les the
l'avion the aeroplane
excusez-moi excuse me
nous we
nous avons we have
les places the seats
neuf nine
a, b pronounce 'ah', 'bay'
et and
oui yes
un moment a/one moment
s'il vous plait please
bonjour good day, good morning, good afternoon, hello
nous sommes we are
mon, ma, mes my
le nom the name
est is
non no
malheureusement unfortunately
je I
je suis I am
nous allons we go, we are going
à to, at
vous you (polite)
aussi also, too
je vais I go, I am going
mais but
de of, from
j'étais I was
en in, at
mai May
très very
beau, belle beautiful
une ville a town
pour for
le travail the work
que what
que faites-vous? what do you do?
je travaille I work
avec with
(des) ordinateurs computers
madame Mrs
chez at
actuellement now, at present
c'est it is, this is
mieux better
vous êtes you are (polite)
nous étions we were
un, une a
un an, les ans a year, the years
trois three
avez-vous? do you have? (polite)
bon, bonne good
un poste a post, position, job
la banque the bank
ne... pas not
intéressant(e) interesting
bien payé well paid
j'ai I have
j'ai besoin de I have need of, I need
beaucoup (de) much, a lot (of)
l'argent, d'argent the money, of money
grand(e) big
une maison a house

quatre four
les enfants the children
la femme the wife, woman
américain(e) American
elle she, it
a has
ses parents his/her parents
une amie a girlfriend
toujours always
le/au téléphone the telephone/ on the telephone
ça coûte cher it costs a lot
les vacances the holidays
sont are
septembre September
sans without
le (téléphone) portable the mobile (phone)

TOTAL NEW WORDS: 81
... only 308 words to go!

Some extra words

Les mois (the months)

janvier	**avril**	**juillet**	**octobre**
février	**mai**	**août**	**novembre**
mars	**juin**	**septembre**	**décembre**

Les numéros (numbers)

zéro,	**un,**	**deux,**	**trois,**	**quatre,**	**cinq,**	**six,**	**sept,**	**huit,**	**neuf,**	**dix**
0	**1**	**2**	**3**	**4**	**5**	**6**	**7**	**8**	**9**	**10**

More greetings

salut *hi*
allô *hello! (on the telephone)*
Ça va? *How are you?*
bonsoir *good evening*
bonne nuit *good night*
au revoir *goodbye*

Good news grammar

🔊 CD1, tr 4

This is the good news part of each week. Remember, I promised: no confusing grammar! I simply explain the differences between English and French. This will help you to speak French easily.

1 Names of things – nouns

There are two kinds of nouns in French: *masculine* and *feminine*.

You can tell which is which by the word **le** or **la** (*the*), or **un** or **une** (*a* or *one*) in front of the word. ***Le* poste** or ***un* poste** is masculine. ***La* maison** or ***une* maison** is feminine.

If you add an adjective to describe the job or the house, the adjective also becomes masculine or feminine. This means that there can be at least two versions of every adjective.

Le poste est *bon*.	*The job is good.*
une *bonne* maison	*a good house*

Other examples are: **cher** and **chère, grand** and **grande, intéressant** and **intéressante**. But it's **beau** and **belle.**

As you can see, it's not that bad. You usually just add an **e** if the noun starts with **la** or **une.**

When talking about more than one thing, you use **les** and add an **s** to the noun and adjectives: **Les postes sont bons. Les maisons sont bonnes.**

Confused? Here is the Good News: in **Traveller's French** mistakes are allowed. If you say **le maison est grand**, instead of **la maison est grande**, nobody will mind.

2 Doing things – verbs

This is a bit of 'bad news' in French, so brace yourself. When you want to say in French: *I work*, *you work*, *we work*, *he works* or *they work*, the ending of the word **travailler** *to work* changes almost every time. And worse: some verbs change altogether. If you want to say: *I have*, *you have*, or *we have* – it's a completely different word every time.

But don't despair. Start off with learning **travailler** which is a regular paid-up member of the Good Verbs Team (**-er** verbs). These verbs all share the same endings, so know one, know lots.

Next learn **avoir** *to have*. You'll use it every day.

travailler – *(to) work*	
je travaille	*I work*
vous travaillez	*you work*
nous travaillons	*we work*
il travaille	*he, it works*
elle travaille	*she, it works*
ils/elles travaillent	*they work*

avoir – *(to) have*	
j'ai	*I have*
vous avez	*you have*
nous avons	*we have*
il a	*he, it has*
elle a	*she, it has*
ils/elles ont	*they have*

In spoken French, **travaille** and **travaillent** sound the same, so just remember **travaillons** and **travaillez**: easy!

Il and **elle** can both mean *it*: **Le poste – il est bon. La maison – elle est bonne.** *It is good*, in each case.

3 How to say 'not'

When you want to say *not* in French, for example, *I am **not** in Paris*, you use two words: **ne** and **pas**.

You wrap them around your verb, **ne** in front and **pas** behind it: **Je *ne* suis *pas* à Paris.** *I am not in Paris.* **Le travail *n'est pas* intéressant.** *Work isn't interesting.*

Pronunciation

🔊 CD1, tr 5

French pronunciation is very different from English pronunciation and quite complicated, so you really need the recording. It makes learning far easier and you'll be speaking French much faster.

But perhaps you just need a refresher – so here come the rules.

1 Single vowels

The English word in brackets gives you an example of the sound. Say the sound out loud, and then the French examples out loud.

Remember with **Traveller's French**: near enough is good enough.

a	*(cat)*	**à, place, quatre**
e	*(her)*	**le, je**
e, ê, è	*(yes)*	**elle, êtes, très**
é	*(say)*	**étais**
i, y	*(fee)*	**Nice, dix, avril, y**
o	*(not)*	**sommes, poste**
u	*(phew)*	**une, excusez**

2 Doubles and triples

These make only one sound.

ai, aî, ei	*(say)*	**maison, j'ai, mais, faites, étais, plaît, neige** *(snow)*
au, eau, ô	*(no)*	**au, aussi, beau, Renault, côte**
eu	*(curve)*	**deux, ordinateur, malheureusement**
ou, aoû	*(Peru)*	**nous, pour, bonjour, Toulouse, août**

3 Now some vowel combinations

These are pronounced all at once.

oi	*(No-ah)*	**moi, trois, revoir**
oui	*(wee)*	**oui**
ui	*('oo-ee')*	**suis** *(If you say this quickly, it sounds like 'swee'.)*
ieu	*(yer)*	**mieux**

4 Vowel and consonant combinations: *er* and *ez*

You will meet them at the end of words. They are pronounced as one sound, like 'ay' in *play*. The r and z are not pronounced. Now say: aller, chez, excusez.

5 Here come some 'unusuals'

These are unusual because they are said as if you have a cold, and your nose is blocked. They are mostly found at the end of words.

an, en, am, em	*('-arng')*	**dans, moment, septembre**
in, im	*(sang)*	**cardin, cinq**
on, om	*(song)*	**bon, bonjour, nom, allons, maison**
un, um	*('-urng')*	**un**

6 A few consonants

These consonants are different in French.

ç	this strange letter sounds like a double *s* **garçon**
h	this is silent **mal(h)eureusement, (h)omme**
j, g	like *g* in *mirage* **j'ai, jour, Peugeot**
ll	like *y* in *yes* **travaille**
qu	like *k* in *king* **que, banque, quatre**
s	sometimes soft like an English *z* **maison**
ch	like *sh* in *ship* **chez**
r	a dry, 'throaty' version of the English *r* **trois**

7 Finally, silent endings

This is where French is very different from other European languages. Quite a lot of it is not pronounced. Whenever you come across the following letters, usually at the end of a word – just swallow them. They must not be heard.

s	Silent at the end of many French words. Look at these: **dans, avons, vous, suis, Paris, mais, trois** and **toujours**.
t, ts	Both are silent at the end of a word: **et, sont, enfants.** Note: in **est** both **s** and **t** are silent; just pronounce the **e**.
z, x	Both are silent at the end of a word: **chez, beaux, mieux.**
es	Both are silent: **places, sommes, faites, vacances**. But in **les, des** and **très** only the **s** is silent. Say: 'lay', 'day', 'tray'.
e	Many words end in silent **e: appelle, belle, femme.** But **e** is heard when it has an accent (**terminé**) and in words of one syllable: **de, je, le.**

8 Why French sounds 'smooth'

This is because those silent letters at the end of words are pulled across to the next word if it begins with a vowel. So **nous avons** will sound like 'nousavons'. Here are three more examples: **vous aussi, trois ans, nous allons.**

Many words are contracted. When two vowels collide, one is dropped: **je étais** becomes **j'étais** and **ce est** becomes **c'est. C'est si bon!**

You have just studied 50 sounds and 10 exceptions, and you are entitled to be totally exhausted and a little confused. Please listen to the recording – it will really help.

Let's speak French

🔊 CD1, tr 6

Here are ten English sentences for you to put into French. Always speak out loud. After each one check the answer on the next page. Tick it if you got it right. You can check your answers on the recording.

1 My name is Walker.
2 You are from London?
3 Yes, I am from London.
4 I have a girlfriend in Nice.
5 We are going to Toulouse.
6 Do you have a Mercedes?
7 No, unfortunately (not).
8 We have a house in Calais.
9 The work is well paid.
10 You are on holiday?

Well, how many did you get right? If you are not happy, do the exercise again.

Here are some questions in French. Answer each one in French out loud, checking as you go. Start every answer with **oui** and **nous**.

11 Vous êtes de Manchester?
12 Vous avez une maison à Londres?
13 Vous avez besoin d'un poste?
14 Vous travaillez en France?
15 Vous avez quatre enfants?

Now start all your answers with **je** and tell me in French that…

16 you were in Paris in May.
17 you work at Rover.
18 you need a bank.
19 you are not from Toulouse.
20 you don't have a lot of money.

Well, what was your score? If it was 18 or more you should be very pleased with yourself.

Answers

1 Mon nom est Walker.
2 Vous êtes de Londres?
3 Oui, je suis de Londres.
4 J'ai une amie à Nice.
5 Nous allons à Toulouse.
6 Avez-vous une Mercédès? or: Vous avez une Mercédès?
7 Non, malheureusement.
8 Nous avons une maison à Calais.
9 Le travail est bien payé.
10 Vous êtes en vacances?
11 Oui, nous sommes de Manchester.
12 Oui, nous avons une maison à Londres.
13 Oui, nous avons besoin d'un poste.
14 Oui, nous travaillons en France.
15 Oui, nous avons quatre enfants.
16 J'étais à Paris en mai.
17 Je travaille chez Rover.
18 J'ai besoin d'une banque.
19 Je ne suis pas de Toulouse.
20 Je n'ai pas beaucoup d'argent.

Let's speak more French

🔊 CD1, tr 7

Here are some optional exercises. They may stretch the 35 minutes a day by 15 minutes. But the extra practice will be worth it. And always remember: near enough is good enough!

In your own words

This exercise will teach you to express yourself freely. Use only the words you have learned so far.

Tell me in your own words that...

... you are Peter Smith Je suis Peter Smith.

1. you are from Manchester
2. you have an American friend
3. you are a workaholic...
4. but you don't have a lot of cash
5. you have two children
6. the children are six and eight (have six and eight years)
7. unfortunately you work with a PC; the work is not interesting
8. your wife works for a bank in Bath
9. you own a property in Grenoble
10. your children are in Paris

Answers

1. **Je suis de Manchester.**
2. **J'ai un ami américain (m.)/une amie américaine (f.).**
3. **Je travaille beaucoup...**
4. **mais je n'ai pas beaucoup d'argent.**
5. **J'ai deux enfants.**
6. **Les enfants ont six et huit ans.**
7. **Malheureusement je travaille avec un ordinateur; le travail n'est pas intéressant.**
8. **Ma femme travaille pour une banque à Bath.**
9. **J'ai une maison à Grenoble.**
10. **Mes enfants sont à Paris.**

Let's speak French – fast and fluently

CD1, tr 8

No more stuttering and stumbling. Get out the stopwatch and time yourself with this fluency practice.

Translate each section and check if it is correct, then cover up the answers and say the three or four sentences fast. If you manage to say each section in less than 20 seconds you are doing very well.

Some of the English is in 'French-speak' to help you.

Good evening. I am going to Bordeaux. You, too?
No, I work in Perpignan – for a bank. But I am going to Calais.
I am on holiday – without (my) computer.

Bonsoir. Je vais à Bordeaux. Vous aussi?
Non, je travaille à Perpignan – pour une banque. Mais je vais à Calais.
Je suis en vacances – sans ordinateur.

Nice is a beautiful town?
Yes, but it (she) is not big.
It (she) is very interesting.
A house in Nice, that costs a lot of money.

Nice est une belle ville?
Oui, mais elle n'est pas grande.
Elle est très intéressante.
Une maison à Nice, ça coûte beaucoup d'argent.

I have a girlfriend, Julie.
She has a house in Nice.
Oh, excuse me. One moment, please, it is Julie.
She is always on the phone. Bye!

J'ai une amie, Julie.
Elle a une maison à Nice.
Oh, excusez-moi. Un moment, s'il vous plaît, c'est Julie.
Elle est toujours au téléphone. Au revoir!

Learn by heart

🔊 CD1, tr 9

Don't skip this exercise because it reminds you of school. If you want to **speak**, not stumble, learning by heart does the trick! Fill in the gaps with your personal, or any, information.

Mon nom est...

Mon nom est .... (name). Je suis de .... (place).
J'étais à .... (place) en .... (month).
Je travaille chez .... (name of firm).
Nous avons une belle maison à .... (place).
C'est très cher.
En juillet nous allons à .... (place).
Êtes-vous aussi en vacances? Non, malheureusement.

Say **Mon nom est...** out loud and fairly fast. Can you beat 40 seconds?

Test your progress

Translate these sentences into French. This is your only written exercise for the week. You'll be amazed how easy it is! Are you going for 90%?

1 Hello, we are Helen and Paul.
2 I am from Marseille. You, too?
3 I was in Cannes in July.
4 My parents have a Rover.
5 We are going to Nice with the Renault and five children.
6 I don't have a good job.
7 I need a house for the holidays.
8 What do you do? You work with computers?
9 She has two jobs and three telephones.
10 Excuse me, are you Mrs Cardin?
11 We work at Renault. The work is well paid.
12 We have a very expensive computer.
13 I am in France, but without my wife.
14 We were seven months in Paris. That's a lot!
15 I go to Nice in April. It is a beautiful town.

You will find the scoring instructions and answers in the **Answers** section. When you have worked out your result, enter it on the **Progress chart** at the front of the book.

Week 2

Day-by-day guide

35 minutes a day – but a little extra will speed up your progress!

Day one

- Read **In Provence**.
- Listen to/Read **En Provence**.
- Listen to/Read the **New words**. Learn 20 easy ones.

Day two

- Repeat **En Provence** and the **New words**.
- Repeat **Pronunciation**, if you need to.
- Learn the harder **New words**.
- Use the **Flash words** to help you.

Day three

- Learn all the **New words** until you know them well.
- Read and learn the **Good news grammar**.

Day four

- Cut out and learn the ten **Flash sentences**.
- Listen to/Read **Learn by heart**.

Day five

- Listen to/Read **Let's speak French**.
- Go over **Learn by heart**.

Day six

- Listen to/Read **Let's speak more French** (optional).
- Listen to/Read **Let's speak French – fast and fluently** (optional).
- Translate **Test your progress**.

Day seven is a work-free day!

In Provence

Tom and Kate hire a car and head off to Provence. They look for somewhere to stay.

Kate Good afternoon. Have you a room for two for one night and not very expensive, please?

Hotelier Yes, we have a little room with bath. But the shower is broken. Perhaps my husband can it repair.

Tom Where is the room?

Hotelier It is here on the left. Is it that it is enough big?

Kate The room is a little small but not bad. It is how much?

Hotelier Only €45 for two but no credit card, please. There is a breakfast from 8 to 9 hours and half.

Kate All right, we take the room, but can we take the breakfast at 8 o'clock less the quarter? We would like to go tomorrow at 8 o'clock and quarter to Nice.

Tom Another question, where can we take a coffee? Is there a café or a bistro around here?

Hotelier There is a café at five minutes. It is not difficult – 30 metres to the right and then straight ahead.

(In the café)

Waiter What would you like?

Kate A white coffee and a tea with milk, please.

Waiter Would you like to eat something? We have cakes.

Tom Two, please. One with and one without cream.

Tom My tea is cold.

Kate But the coffee is superb.

Tom The table is too small.

Kate But the toilets are very clean.

Tom My cake is not good.

Kate But the waiter is gorgeous.

Tom The bill, please.

Waiter €10.60, please.

En Provence

🔊 CD1, tr 10

Tom and Kate hire a car and head off to Provence. They look for somewhere to stay.

Kate Bonjour. Avez-vous une chambre pour deux pour une nuit et pas très chère, s'il vous plaît?

Hotelier Oui, nous avons une petite chambre avec bain. Mais la douche est en panne. Peut-être mon mari peut la réparer.

Tom Où est la chambre?

Hotelier Elle est ici, à gauche. Est-ce qu'elle est assez grande?

Kate La chambre est un peu petite mais pas mal. C'est combien?

Hotelier Seulement quarante-cinq euros pour deux, mais pas de carte de crédit, s'il vous plaît. Il y a un petit déjeuner de huit à neuf heures et demie.

Kate D'accord, nous prenons la chambre. Mais pouvons-nous prendre le petit déjeuner à huit heures moins le quart? Nous voudrions aller demain à huit heures et quart à Nice.

Tom Une autre question, où pouvons-nous prendre un café? Il y a un café ou un bistrot par ici?

Hotelier Il y a un café à cinq minutes. Ce n'est pas difficile – trente mètres à droite et ensuite tout droit.

(Dans le café)

Waiter Que désirez-vous?

Kate Un café crème et un thé au lait, s'il vous plaît.

Waiter Vous désirez manger quelque chose? Nous avons des gâteaux.

Tom Deux, s'il vous plaît. Un avec et un sans crème fraîche.

Tom Mon thé est froid.

Kate Mais le café est superbe.

Tom La table est trop petite.

Kate Mais les toilettes sont très propres.

Tom Mon gâteau n'est pas bon.

Kate Mais le serveur est adorable.

Tom L'addition, s'il vous plaît.

Waiter Dix euros soixante centimes, s'il vous plaît.

New words

🔊 CD1, tr 11

la chambre the room
la nuit the night
(ne)... pas, pas de no, not
petit(e) small
le bain the bath
la douche the shower
en panne broken down, not working
peut-être perhaps, *lit*. can be
le mari the husband
il peut he can
la (on its own) her, it
réparer to repair
où? where?
ici, par ici here, around here
à gauche on the left
est-ce que...? is it that...? (used to start a question)
assez (de) enough (of)
un peu a little
pas mal not bad
combien? how much, how many?
seulement only
quarante 40
la carte de crédit the credit card
il y a there is, there are
le petit déjeuner the breakfast
de...à from...to
huit eight
neuf heures nine hours, nine o'clock
et demie and half, half past
d'accord all right, agreed
nous prenons we take
nous pouvons we can
prendre to take
moins less
moins le quart *lit*. less the quarter, quarter to
nous voudrions we would like
aller to go
demain tomorrow
et quart and quarter, quarter past
autre other
la question the question
le café the coffee, the café
la minute the minute
difficile difficult
trente 30
à droite on the right
ensuite then, next, finally
tout droit straight ahead
le serveur the waiter
vous désirez you would like
le café crème the white coffee
le thé the tea
au lait with milk
manger to eat
quelque chose something
le gâteau, des gateaux the cake, cakes
ou or
la crème (fraîche) the cream
froid(e) cold
superbe super, superb
la table the table
trop too
trop de ... too much, too many ...
les toilettes the toilets
propre clean
adorable adorable, gorgeous
l'addition the bill
soixante 60
le centime the cent (part of euro)

TOTAL NEW WORDS: 69
... only 239 words to go!

Some useful extras

Les numéros *(numbers)*

11	**onze**
12	**douze**
13	**treize**
14	**quatorze**
15	**quinze**
16	**seize**
17	**dix-sept** *(ten-seven)*
18	**dix-huit** *(ten-eight)*
19	**dix-neuf** *(ten-nine)*
20	**vingt**
21	**vingt et un**
22	**vingt-deux**
23	**vingt-trois**
30	**trente**
40	**quarante**
50	**cinquante**
60	**soixante**
70	**soixante-dix (60 + 10)**
71	**soixante et onze (60 + 11)**
80	**quatre-vingts (4 × 20)**
90	**quatre-vingt-dix (4 × 20 + 10)**
100	**cent**

L'heure *(time, hour)*

à quelle heure?	*at what time?*
à ... heure/s	*at ... o'clock*
une minute	*a minute*
une heure	*an hour*
un jour	*a day*
une semaine	*a week*
un mois	*a month*
un an	*a year*
ce matin	*this morning*
ce soir	*this evening*

21, 31, 41, 51, 61, 71 all get an extra **et**: *twenty and one*. The numbers in between are just as in English: 47 **quarante-sept**.

Here are two important verb boxes. But don't worry about them today. They are for tomorrow when you've read the **Good news grammar**.

être – *to be*	
je suis	*I am*
vous êtes	*you are*
nous sommes	*we are*
il est	*he is, it is*
elle est	*she is, it is*
ils/elles sont	*they are*

aller – *to go*	
je vais	*I go*
vous allez	*you go*
nous allons	*we go*
il va	*he goes, it goes*
elle va	*she goes, it goes*
ils/elles vont	*they go*

Good news grammar

🔊 CD1, tr 12

1 Asking questions – that's easy!

To ask a question in French you can use your voice to change **Vous avez un bon poste!** into **Vous avez un bon poste?** Or you can turn the words around: **Avez-vous** un bon poste? Put a hyphen in between if you are writing.

You can also start a question using **Est-ce que**. It literally means: *Is it that…?* So you haven't got anywhere except gaining a bit of time for your question. **Est-ce que** (..um..) **vous avez un bain?** If you don't want a mouth full of teeth say: **Vous avez un bain?** It's much easier.

2 *Il y a:* there is, there are

You will use this a lot:

***Il y a* un petit déjeuner superbe.**
***Il y a* des gâteaux au chocolat.**

If you want to ask *is there?* or *are there?* you can either stay with **il y a?**, using your voice to make it sound like a question, or turn it around and say y **a-t-il?**

***Il y a* un café par ici? *Y a-t-il* un café par ici?**

If you go for the second option you slot in the **t** to make it sound better.

3 Du, de la, de l', des

These are used when you don't want to say *the cakes* or *the coffee*, but simply *cakes* or *coffee*. So you would say: **des gâteaux** or **du café**.

Also, if you want to say *of the* or *from the*, you use these, e.g. **de la banque** *of/from the bank*, **de l'hôtel** *from the hotel*, **des enfants** *of the children*.

4 C'est

This pops up frequently. Remember: **c'est** means both *it is* and *this/that is*:

C'est combien? **C'est bon!**

5 *Être* and *aller* – you'll use these every day

Think how often you say *I am…* or *we are going…* I have put the verbs **être** and **aller** into boxes for you. They are in the **Some useful extras** section. Spend five minutes on each of them now.

Let's speak French

🔊 CD1, tr 13

If you have the recording, use it to check your answers. Here are ten sentences for you to say in French out loud.

1 Do you have a double room?
2 Do you have the bill, please?
3 At what time is breakfast?
4 The telephone is broken.
5 Can he repair it?
6 We would like to eat something.
7 Where is the café, on the left or on the right?
8 How much is it?
9 We take it.
10 I work from 9 o'clock to 6 (18) o'clock.

Now answer these questions. Use **oui** where you can:

11 La chambre est assez grande?
12 La chambre, c'est combien, 30 euros?
13 La Peugeot est en panne?
14 Il y a un téléphone par ici?

Answer these questions with **non**. Use **je** and **ne pas**.

15 Vous travaillez chez Rover?
16 Vous êtes serveur?
17 Avez-vous une grande Mercédès?

Now give your own answers. Don't worry if mine are different. Yours could still be correct.

18 Où allez-vous?
19 À quelle heure désirez-vous manger?
20 Où est l'hôtel La Belle Provence?

Answers

1 Vous avez une chambre pour deux?
2 Vous avez l'addition, s'il vous plaît?/Avez-vous...?
3 C'est à quelle heure le petit déjeuner?
4 Le téléphone est en panne.
5 Peut-il le réparer?
6 Nous voudrions manger quelque chose.
7 Où est le café, à gauche ou à droite?
8 C'est combien?
9 Nous le/la prenons.
10 Je travaille de neuf heures à dix-huit heures.
11 Oui, la chambre est assez grande.
12 Oui, la chambre est à trente euros.
13 Oui, la Peugeot est en panne.
14 Oui, il y a un téléphone par ici.
15 Non, je ne travaille pas chez Rover.
16 Non, je ne suis pas serveur.
17 Non, je n'ai pas une grande Mercédès.
18 Nous allons à Paris.
19 Nous voudrions manger à huit heures.
20 L'hôtel La Belle Provence est en Provence.

Let's speak more French

🔊 CD1, tr 14

Here are the two optional exercises. Remember, they may stretch the 35 minutes a day by 15 minutes. But the extra practice will be worth it.

In your own words

This exercise will teach you to express yourself freely. Use only the words you have learned so far.

Ask me in your own words...

1 if an en suite double room is available
2 what the price of the room is for one night
3 where you can have a coffee

Tell me...

4 that there is a café 20 minutes away; you go straight ahead
5 you would like (the) breakfast at 7.30
6 you are thinking of driving to Carcassonne the next day
7 you want coffee and cakes
8 what you don't like about the café
9 what Kate likes about the café (*dit* (says:...))
10 that the bill is €9.60

Answers

1 Avez-vous une chambre pour deux avec bain ou douche?
2 C'est combien la chambre pour une nuit?
3 Où y a-t-il un café par ici?
4 Il y a un café à vingt minutes. Vous allez tout droit.
5 Nous voudrions le petit déjeuner à sept heures et demie.
6 Nous voudrions aller à Carcassonne demain.
7 Nous voudrions du café et des gâteaux.
8 La table est trop petite et le gâteau n'est pas bon.
9 Kate dit: 'Les toilettes sont superbes et le serveur est adorable'.
10 L'addition est neuf euros et soixante centimes.

Let's speak French – fast and fluently

CD1, tr 15

No more stuttering and stumbling! Get out the stopwatch and time yourself with this fluency practice.

Translate each section and check if it is correct, then cover up the answers and say the three or four sentences as quickly as you can.

If you can say each section in less than 20 seconds you are doing very well.

Some of the English is in 'French-speak' to help you.

Good evening, do you have a room with bath?
80 euros is a little expensive.
We would like a room with shower.
It is how much, the breakfast? We can it **(le)** *take at 7 o'clock?*

Bonsoir, avez-vous une chambre avec bain?
Quatre-vingts euros est un peu cher.
Nous voudrions une chambre avec douche.
C'est combien, le petit déjeuner? Nous pouvons le prendre à sept heures?

Where is my house? Straight ahead, then you go to the right.
But we are going tomorrow to Montpellier.
We would like to go to Montpellier at 9 hours and half.

Où est ma maison? Tout droit, ensuite vous allez à droite.
Mais demain nous allons à Montpellier.
Nous voudrions aller à Montpellier à neuf heures et demie.

The café here is very small and very expensive.
But the coffee is good, and the cakes are excellent.
The bill, please. How much? 38 euros for two coffees and two cakes?
We do not have enough money.

Le café ici est très petit et très cher.
Mais le café est bon, et les gâteaux sont superbes.
L'addition, s'il vous plaît. Combien? Trente-huit euros pour deux cafés et deux gâteaux?
Nous n'avons pas assez d'argent.

Now say all the sentences in French without stopping and starting. Try to stay them in under a minute. You did? Great!

Learn by heart

🔊 CD1, tr 16

Learn the following lines by heart. When you know them say them fast and with a bit of drama. Use the name of a friend after **avec**.

Je n'ai pas beaucoup d'argent, mais...

Je n'ai pas beaucoup d'argent,
mais je voudrais aller en vacances avec ...
Nous voudrions aller à St Tropez. Nous prenons la Renault.
Il y a beaucoup de petits hôtels pas chers.
Malheureusement ce n'est pas possible.
Il y a toujours trop de travail
et... la Renault est en panne!

Test your progress

Translate the following sentences and write them down. Resist the temptation of looking back at previous pages.

1 We would like to have (take) a coffee.
2 Is there a bank around here?
3 We are going to eat something.
4 Do you have the bill for the tea, please?
5 My children do not have enough (of) money.
6 Where is the room?
7 They always go to the (*au*) café at half past six.
8 Another question please: where are the toilets, straight ahead?
9 You are going to Oslo in January?
10 She goes to Los Angeles with her husband.
11 The breakfast is great. How much is it?
12 Where are you tomorrow at half past ten?
13 There is a bank on the left.
14 I am going on holiday in July.
15 Excuse me, we only have a credit card.
16 All right, we'll take the Renault for two days.
17 We are going to repair the Citroën. It has broken down.
18 I work 12 hours. We need money.
19 €3 for a cold tea? That's too much!
20 There are 40 cafés around here, one (at) two minutes from here.

Check your answers in the **Answers** section. The **Progress chart** awaits your score.

Week 3

Day-by-day guide

Study for 35 minutes a day – but there are no penalties for doing more.

Day one

- Read **We are going shopping.**
- Listen to/Read **Nous allons faire les courses.**
- Read the **New words**, then learn some of them.

Day two

- Repeat the story and **New words.**
- Learn all the **New words**. Use the Flash words!

Day three

- Test yourself on all the **New words** – Boring, boring, but you are over half way already!
- Have a first look at **Learn by heart**.
- Learn the **Good news grammar**.

Day four

- Cut out and learn the **Flash sentences.**
- Listen to/Read **Learn by heart.**

Day five

- Listen to/Read **Let's speak French**.
- Listen to/Read **Spot the keys.**

Day six

- Listen to/Read **Let's speak more French** (optional).
- Listen to/Read **Let's speak French – fast and fluently** (optional).
- Have a quick look at the **New words** Weeks 1–3. You know 225 words by now! ... well, give or take a few.
- Translate **Test your progress**.

Day seven – **Enjoy your day off!**

We're going shopping

Next stop Nice and a week in a holiday apartment. Kate wants to go shopping but Tom is less than keen.

Kate Today we must do the shopping. We are going to take the bus for the town centre.

Tom But the weather is bad. It makes cold and there is sport on the television... golf at one o'clock and half.

Kate I am sorry but we must first go to the cashpoint machine of the bank, then to the post office to buy stamps and afterwards, to the chemist's and to the dry cleaner's.

Tom So, no golf... perhaps football at three o'clock. That is all for the shopping?

Kate No, I must go in a department store, to the supermarket and to the hairdresser. And afterwards in a shoe-shop.

Tom My God! The shops are open until what hour?

Kate Until 7 o'clock, I believe.

Tom Well, no football... but perhaps tennis at seven o'clock and quarter.

(Later)

Kate I believe that I have bought too many things: bread, a half kilo of cheese, 200 grams of ham, potatoes, butter, eggs, sugar, six bottles of beer and a bottle of wine.

Tom That's all right. No problem. It's enough for tomorrow. We have not much eaten yesterday. What is it that this is? What is it that there is in the big bag? Is it for me?

Kate Well, I was at the hairdresser's at Galeries Lafayette and I have seen shoes exactly at my size. They are super, no? Blue with white. The sales assistant was very nice and gorgeous, like Tom Cruise.

Tom Who is Tom Cruise? And how much the shoes?

Kate They were a little expensive, but the same price as in England... €150.

Tom What? But this is a price mad!

Kate But this t-shirt of golf was very cheap, in size 44, only €15, and I have bought a newspaper English and... is there not tennis on the television now?

Nous allons faire les courses

CD1, tr 17

Next stop Nice and a week in a holiday apartment. Kate wants to go shopping but Tom is less than keen.

Kate Aujourd'hui nous devons faire les courses. Nous allons prendre le bus pour le centre ville.

Tom Mais le temps est mauvais. Il fait froid et il y a du sport à la télé... du golf, à une heure et demie.

Kate Je suis désolée mais nous devons d'abord aller au distributeur de la banque, ensuite à la poste acheter des timbres et après, à la pharmacie et au pressing.

Tom Alors, pas de golf... peut-être du football à trois heures. C'est tout pour les courses?

Kate Non, je dois aller dans un grand magasin, au supermarché et chez le coiffeur. Et après, dans un magasin de chaussures.

Tom Mon Dieu! Les magasins sont ouverts jusqu'à quelle heure?

Kate Jusqu'à sept heures, je crois.

Tom Alors, pas de football... mais peut-être du tennis à sept heures et quart.

(Plus tard)

Kate Je crois que j'ai acheté trop de choses: du pain, un demi kilo de fromage, 200 grammes de jambon, des pommes de terre, du beurre, des oeufs, du sucre, six bouteilles de bière et une bouteille de vin.

Tom C'est bien. Pas de problème. C'est assez pour demain. Nous n'avons pas beaucoup mangé hier. Qu'est-ce que c'est? Qu'est-ce qu'il y a dans le grand sac? C'est pour moi?

Kate Alors, j'étais chez le coiffeur aux Galeries Lafayette et j'ai vu des chaussures exactement à ma taille. Elles sont superbes, non? Du bleu avec du blanc. Le vendeur était très sympathique et adorable comme Tom Cruise.

Tom Qui est Tom Cruise? Et combien les chaussures?

Kate Elles étaient un peu chères, mais le même prix qu'en Angleterre... cent cinquante euros.

Tom Quoi? Mais c'est un prix fou!

Kate Mais ce tee-shirt de golf était très bon marché, en taille quarante-quatre, seulement quinze euros, et j'ai acheté un journal anglais et... il n'y a pas de tennis à la télé maintenant?

New words

🔊 CD1, tr 18

Learn the **New words** in half the time by using the **Flash cards**. There are 22 to start you off.

faire to do, make
faire les courses to do the shopping
aujourd'hui today
nous devons we must
le bus the bus
le centre ville the town centre
le temps the weather
mauvais(e) bad
il fait froid it is (*lit*. makes) cold
la télé(vision) the TV
je suis désolé(e) I am sorry
d'abord first
le distributeur (automatique) the cashpoint machine
la poste the post office
acheter to buy
les timbres the stamps
après afterwards, later
la pharmacie the chemist's
le pressing the dry cleaner's
alors so, then
tout(e) all
je dois I must
le grand magasin the department store
le supermarché the supermarket
le coiffeur the hairdresser
le magasin the shop
les chaussures the shoes
Mon Dieu! My God!
ouvert(e) open
jusqu'à until
je crois I believe
plus more
plus tard later
j'ai acheté I have bought, I bought
les choses the things
le pain the bread
un demi kilo half a kilo
le fromage the cheese
le jambon the ham
les pommes de terre the potatoes
le beurre the butter
les oeufs the eggs
le sucre the sugar
la bouteille the bottle
la bière the beer
le vin the wine
c'est bien that's all right
pas de problème no problem
nous avons mangé we have eaten, we ate
hier yesterday
qu'est-ce que…? what? *lit*. what is it that…?
qu'est-ce qu'il y a? what is there?/ what is the matter?
le sac the bag
moi me
Galeries Lafayette chain of department stores
j'ai vu I have seen, I saw
exactement exactly
à ma taille in my size
bleu(e) blue
blanc blanche white
le vendeur the sales assistant
il était, ils étaient he was, they were
sympathique nice, pleasant

comme like, also: how
qui who
le, la même ... que the same ... as
le prix the price
Angleterre England
quoi what
fou, folle mad, crazy
ce, cette this
bon marché cheap
le journal the newspaper
anglais(e) English
maintenant now

TOTAL NEW WORDS: 75
... only 164 words to go!

Some easy extras

Les couleurs (the colours)

blanc, blanche white
noir, noire black
rouge red
bleu, bleue blue
vert, verte green
jaune yellow
brun, brune, marron brown
gris, grise grey
orange orange
rose pink

Spend five minutes learning **devoir** and perhaps another five tomorrow.

devoir – *must*

je dois	*I must*
vous devez	*you must*
nous devons	*we must*
il doit	*he, it must*
elle doit	*she, it must*
ills/elles doivent	*they must*

Learn by heart

CD1, tr 19

Say these seven lines in under a minute. The more expression you use the easier it will be to remember all the useful bits later.

Pas de problème!

Aujourd'hui nous devons faire les courses – pas de problème!
Alors, nous prenons le bus pour le centre ville.
Mon Dieu! Je crois que je n'ai pas assez d'argent.
Où y a-t-il un distributeur?
Je suis désolée, j'ai trop acheté: du pain, du beurre, du jambon et du fromage, et cinq bouteilles de vin rouge...
Mais le vendeur était adorable!

Good news grammar

CD1, tr 20

1 The past

When you talk about something that happened earlier, or in the past, in French you usually use **avoir** plus the other verb, slightly changed. Remember **travailler**, a regular verb with nice regular endings? If you want to say in French that you *have worked*, or that *you worked*, you would **say j'ai travaillé**. If you *have bought* something you would say **j'ai acheté**, and if someone *repaired* something, you would say **il a réparé**. Every time, the **-er** ending of the main verb changes to **-é**.

Unfortunately some verbs have their very own words for the past. For example: **prendre** becomes **pris** (*taken*) and **faire** becomes **fait** (*made*, *done*). When you learn your **New words** in Weeks 4, 5 and 6, you'll often find the past next to it, like this: **je connais/connu** *I know/ known*. You can then 'mix and match' by yourself:

Je *connais* Yvette. Nous avons *connu Pierre*.

Was and *were* are different, remember? **était, étaient**

Le vendeur *était* comme Tom Cruise.
Les chaussures *étaient un peu chères*.

Have a sneak preview of the verbs in Week 6.

2 *Aller à, aller dans, aller chez:* three ways to say 'going to ...'

Don't panic. You can use **aller à** most of the time. If you are going to an office or a shop and use **aller à**, it would be a quick pit-stop. When you use **aller dans**, it means that you are spending time inside, like in a store. And you use **aller chez** when you are calling on a particular person there.

Remember Kate? She went to the post office, the department store and the hairdresser's: ***à* la poste, *dans* un grand magasin** and ***chez* le coiffeur**. But if you muddle them up there are no penalties.

3 *Qu'est-ce que c'est?:* What's this? What's that? What is it?

Word for word **Qu'est-ce que c'est** means *what is it that it is?* Talk about making a meal of it. When a French person asks this, it sounds like 'case-ke-say?' Practise saying it as you'll use it a lot.

4 *Qu'est-ce qu'il y a?:* What is there? What is the matter?

Word for word it means *What is it that there is?* Say it fast, 'case-keelia?', and use it!

5 Vin rouge, journal anglais

Except for such frequently used words as **grand, petit** or **bon,** adjectives usually follow the noun. So it's *wine red* and *newspaper English*.

Let's speak French

🔊 CD2, tr 1

Over to you. If you have the recording, use it to check your answers.

Let's start with a ten-point warm up. Say in French:

1 We need €80.
2 We must go to the bank.
3 Who is (who it is) on the TV?
4 Is there a sales assistant here?
5 Are the shops open?
6 They were here from 6 o'clock to 10 o'clock.
7 I must buy something.
8 Is there a bus for the centre?
9 My God, it is cold today!
10 It's too expensive. I'm sorry.

Answer in French using **non** and **nous**:

11 Vous avez vu le football?
12 Vous avez mangé le pâté?
13 Vous avez acheté le journal?
14 Vous avez vu le golf?
15 Vous avez acheté beaucoup de bière?

Now ask some questions in French starting with **qu'est-ce que**. Then answer in French using the word in brackets:

16 What is this? *(my beer)*
17 What is there in the bag? *(potatoes)*
18 What did you buy? *(a newspaper)*
19 What did you see? *(golf on TV)*
20 What did you eat? *(a lot of cheese)*

Answers

1 Nous avons besoin de quatre-vingts euros.
2 Nous devons aller à la banque.
3 Qui c'est à la télé?
4 Il y a un vendeur par ici?
5 Les magasins sont ouverts?
6 Ils étaient ici de six heures à dix heures.
7 Je dois acheter quelque chose.
8 Y a-t-il un bus pour le centre ville?
9 Mon Dieu, aujourd'hui il fait froid!
10 C'est trop cher. Je suis désolé.
11 Non, nous n'avons pas vu le football.
12 Non, nous n'avons pas mangé le pâté.
13 Non, nous n'avons pas acheté le journal.
14 Non, nous n'avons pas vu le golf.
15 Non, nous n'avons pas acheté beaucoup de bière.
16 Qu'est-ce que c'est? C'est ma bière.
17 Qu'est-ce qu'il y a dans le sac? Il y a des pommes de terre dans le sac.
18 Qu'est-ce que vous avez acheté? J'ai acheté un journal.
19 Qu'est-ce que vous avez vu? J'ai vu du golf à la télé.
20 Qu'est-ce que vous avez mangé? J'ai mangé beaucoup de fromage.

Let's speak more French

🔊 CD2, tr 2

For these optional exercises add an extra 15 minutes to your daily schedule.

And remember, don't worry about getting the article or endings wrong. Near enough is good enough.

In your own words

This exercise will teach you to express yourself freely. Use only the words you have learned so far.

Tell me in your own words that…

1. you must go shopping today
2. you are aiming for the middle of the town
3. you are out of cash
4. you have to go first to a cashpoint machine
5. then you have to go to the pharmacy
6. you saw a supermarket but it (he) was not open
7. you have to buy black shoes, size 37
8. you bought the shoes, and they weren't cheap
9. you did not buy much in the supermarket
10. you bought bread and butter, and a little white wine – ten bottles

---

Answers

1. **Je dois aller faire des courses aujourd'hui.**
2. **Je vais au centre ville.**
3. **Je n'ai pas d'argent.**
4. **D'abord je dois aller au distributeur de la banque…**
5. **ensuite je dois aller à la pharmacie.**
6. **J'ai vu un supermarché mais il n'était pas ouvert.**
7. **Je dois acheter des chaussures noires, taille trente-sept.**
8. **J'ai acheté les chaussures, et elles n'étaient pas bon marché.**
9. **Je n'ai pas acheté beaucoup au supermarché.**
10. **J'ai acheté du pain et du beurre, et un peu de vin blanc – dix bouteilles.**

Let's speak French – fast and fluently

🔊 CD2, tr 3

Translate each section and check if it is correct, then cover up the answers and say the three or four sentences fast.

If you can do each section in less than 20 seconds you are doing very well.

Some of the English is in 'French-speak' to help you.

Excuse me, are you buying a mobile phone?
Is it expensive, the blue mobile?
No, not very, in England it is the same price.

Excusez-moi, vous achetez un téléphone portable?
C'est cher, le portable bleu?
Non, pas très, en Angleterre c'est le même prix.

We would like to buy a house.
We have seen a house here, In Cannes.
Is it (she) big?
It (she) is too small and too expensive.

Nous voudrions acheter une maison.
Nous avons vu une maison ici, à Cannes.
Elle est grande?
Elle est trop petite et trop chère.

The weather was cold in April.
I was in Dijon. I ate in the town centre.
The restaurant was very expensive – 300 euros.
But we had a lot of wine. It was wonderful.

Il a fait froid en avril.
J'étais à Dijon. J'ai dîné au centre ville.
Le restaurant était très cher – trois cents euros.
Mais nous avons pris beaucoup de vin. C'était superbe.

Now say all the sentences in French without stopping and starting. Try to say them in under a minute. But if you are not happy with your result – just try once more.

Spot the keys

🔊 CD2, tr 4

By now you can say many things in French. But what happens if you ask a question and do not understand the answer – hitting you at the speed of an automatic rifle? No need to panic. Listen for familiar words – **key words** which tell you what the other person is saying.

If you have the recording, listen to the dialogue, if you don't – read on.

You: **Excusez moi, où est la poste?**

Answer: *Alors, c'esttrèssimple. D'abord* **tout droit jusqu'** *au prochaincroisement, làbasprèsdela* **maison rouge. Ensuite à gauche, il y a** *une résidence du troisième âge et toute une rangée de* **magasins.** *Et immédiatementaprès un* **pressing à droite,** *vousarrivezsurle* **parking de la place de la poste.**

Despite a lot of words running into each other did you spot the key words?

Test your progress

Translate the following sentences and write them down. Then check the answers and be amazed by your progress.

1 Have you seen a sales assistant?
2 At what time must you go to (*en*) town today?
3 Who saw Pierre on the television yesterday?
4 I believe that the shops are open now.
5 Is there a department store around here or in the centre?
6 Excuse me, I must go to the post office. You, too?
7 Where did you buy the English newspaper?
8 The weather is bad today. It is cold.
9 What? Is that all? That was very cheap!
10 A stamp for (the) England – it is how much?
11 I have a credit card. Is there a cashpoint machine?
12 We must go to the dry cleaner's. That's all right, no problem.
13 Do you have a bag for my black shoes, please?
14 I believe I have seen a chemist's around here.
15 Size 12 English – that is what in France?
16 Did you work until 5 o'clock or later?
17 I am sorry, we have eaten all the ham.
18 First I must repair the bag, and then we can do the shopping.
19 We have taken everything: beer, wine and cheese.
20 That was a very nice sales assistant.

Remember to fill in the **Progress chart**.
You are now halfway to speaking **Traveller's French**.

Week 4

Day-by-day guide

Study 35 minutes a day but if you are keen try 40… 45…

Day one

- Read **We are going to eat out**.
- Listen to/Read **Nous allons dîner**.
- Read the **New words**. Learn the easy ones.

Day two

- Repeat the dialogue. Learn the harder **New words**.
- Cut out the **Flash words** to help you.

Day three

- Learn all the **New words** until you know them well.
- Read and learn the **Good news grammar**.

Day four

- Cut out and learn the **Flash sentences**.
- Listen to/Read **Learn by heart**.

Day five

- Read **Say it simply**.
- Listen to/Read **Let's speak French**.

Day six

- Listen to/Read **Let's speak more French** (optional).
- Listen to/Read **Let's speak French – fast and fluently** (optional).
- Listen to/Read **Spot the keys**.
- Translate **Test your progress**.

Day seven

Are you keeping your scores above 60%? In that case, enjoy your day off.

We're going to eat out

No more 'French-speak'. As you'll have realized by now not everything can be translated word for word from one language to the other. If you simply exchange the words people may well understand you and might even be amused. But saying things the French way will sound much better. It will also impress the locals.

Still in Nice, Tom and Kate are off to dinner with an important client. But will Kate be able to handle the infamous Edith?

Kate Somebody has telephoned. He didn't say why. The name and the number are on this (piece of) paper. Mr Durant from Lyon.

Tom Ah yes, Alain Durant. A very good client of the company. I know him well. He is very nice. I have an appointment with him on Thursday. It is a very important matter.
(*On the telephone*) Hello? Good morning, Mr Durant. This is Tom Walker. How are you? Yes, thank you... Yes, sure, that is possible... next week... yes, very interesting... pardon?... no, we have time... super... no, only some days... oh yes... when?... at eight o'clock... upstairs, at the exit... in front of the door. Well, until this evening. Thank you very much and goodbye.

Kate What are we doing this evening?

Tom We are going to have dinner with Mr Durant. In the centre, behind the church. He says that the restaurant is new and very good. Mr Durant is in Nice for two days with Edith and Peter Palmer from the office.

Kate I know Edith Palmer. I do not like her. She is very snobbish and has a horrible dog. I believe I am going to be ill. Flu with headaches. Where is the number of the doctor?

Tom No, that's not possible. Mr Durant is very nice. One cannot do that.

(In the restaurant...)

Waiter We have menus at €30 or at €37.50 or à la carte. The dessert of the day is chocolate mousse with ice cream or cream.

Alain Mrs Walker, can I help you? Perhaps a soup and fish or meat?

Kate A steak with salad, please.

 Edith Too much red meat, it's not good for you, Kate.

Nous allons dîner

🔊 CD2, tr 5

Still in Nice, Tom and Kate are off to dinner with an important client. But will Kate be able to handle the infamous Edith?

Kate Quelqu'un a téléphoné. Il n'a pas dit pourquoi. Le nom et le numéro sont sur ce papier. Monsieur Durant de Lyon.

Tom Ah oui, Alain Durant. Un très bon client du bureau. Je le connais bien. Il est très sympathique. J'ai rendez-vous avec lui jeudi. C'est une affaire très importante. (*Au téléphone*) Allô. Bonjour, Monsieur Durant. Ici Tom Walker. Ça va? Oui, merci... Oui, bien sûr, c'est possible... la semaine prochaine... oui, très intéressant... pardon?... non, nous avons le temps... superbe... non, seulement quelques jours... ah oui... quand?... à huit heures... en haut, à la sortie... devant la porte. Alors, à ce soir. Merci beaucoup et au revoir.

Kate Que faisons-nous ce soir?

Tom Nous allons dîner avec Monsieur Durant. Dans le centre, derrière l'église. Il dit que le restaurant est nouveau et très bon. Monsieur Durant est à Nice pour deux jours avec Edith et Peter Palmer du bureau.

Kate Je connais Edith Palmer. Je ne l'aime pas. Elle est très snob et a un chien horrible! Je crois que je vais être malade. La grippe avec des maux de tête. Où est le numéro du médecin?

Tom Non, ce n'est pas possible. Monsieur Durant est très sympathique. On ne peut pas faire ça.

(Au restaurant…)

Waiter Nous avons des menus à trente euros ou trente-sept euros cinquante ou à la carte. Le dessert du jour, c'est de la mousse au chocolat avec de la glace ou de la crème fraîche.

Alain Madame Walker, puis-je vous aider? Peut-être un potage et un poisson ou une viande?

Kate Un steak avec de la salade, s'il vous plaît.

Edith Trop de viande rouge, ce n'est pas bon pour vous, Kate.

Alain And for you, Mr Walker? What would you like to drink?

Tom Now then, I would like an escalope in cream sauce and some red wine, please.

Edith Tom, there is a lot of cream. That is too much for you.

Alain And you, Mrs. Palmer?

Edith A little grilled chicken, vegetables and a glass of water, please.

(Later)

Alain Has everyone finished? Would you like some fruit, some cheese, some coffee? No, nothing? Nobody? Well then, the bill, please.

Edith Oh, Monsieur Durant, can you help me, please? How do you say 'doggie bag' in French? I would like a plastic bag for my dog.

Kate But Edith, the dog is in England!

Alain Et pour vous, Monsieur Walker? Que désirez-vous boire?

Tom Alors, je voudrais une escalope à la crème et du vin rouge, s'il vous plaît.

Edith Tom, il y a beaucoup de crème. C'est trop pour vous.

Alain Et vous, Madame Palmer?

Edith Un peu de poulet grillé, des légumes et un verre d'eau, s'il vous plaît.

(Plus tard)

Alain Tout le monde a terminé? Vous désirez des fruits, du fromage, du café? Non, rien? Personne? Bien, alors l'addition, s'il vous plaît.

Edith Ah, Monsieur Durant, vous pouvez m'aider, s'il vous plaît? Comment dit-on 'doggie bag' en français? Je voudrais un sac en plastique pour mon chien.

Kate Mais Edith, le chien est en Angleterre!

New words

🔊 CD2, tr 6

dsîner/diné to eat out, dine/eaten out, dined
quelqu'un someone
il a téléphoné he has telephoned
il a dit he has said/said
pourquoi why
le numéro the number
sur on
le papier the paper
un client a client
le bureau the office
le (on its own) him, it
je connais/connu I know/known (a person or place)
bien well
le rendez-vous the meeting
lui him
jeudi Thursday
une affaire a matter
important(e) important
ça va? how are you?
bien sûr sure, of course
possible possible
la semaine week
prochain(e) next
nous avons le temps we have time
quelques jours a few days
quand when
en haut above, upstairs
la sortie the exit
devant in front of
la porte the door
mardi Tuesday
merci merci bien thank you
merci beaucoup thank you very much
nous faisons/fait we do, make/done, made
derrière behind
l'église the church
il dit he says
nouveau, nouvelle new
j'aime I like, love
snob snob snobbish
un chien a dog
horrible horrible
malade ill, sick
la grippe flu
les maux de tête the headaches
le médecin the doctor
le menu the menu
le dessert du jour the dessert of the day
la mousse au chocolat the chocolate mousse
la glace the ice cream
je peux, but: puis-je? I can, can I?
aider/aidé to help/helped
un potage a soup
un poisson a fish
une viande a meat
la salade the salad
boire to drink
alors now then, well
le poulet grillé the grilled chicken
les légumes the vegetables
un verre d'eau a glass of water
tout le monde everyone
terminé(e) finished
les fruits the fruit
rien nothing

personne nobody
vous pouvez m'aider? can you help me?
on one (as in: one should not…)
comment dit-on? how does one say?
en français in French
en plastique plastic

TOTAL NEW WORDS: 71
… only 93 words to go!

Last easy extras

Les jours de la semaine (days of the week)

lundi Monday
mardi Tuesday
mercredi Wednesday
jeudi Thursday
vendredi Friday
samedi Saturday
dimanche Sunday

Good news grammar

🔊 CD2, tr 7

1 The future – easy!

If you want to talk about something that *is going* to happen – later, tomorrow, in the future – you can use **aller**:

Nous *allons* faire les courses.	*We are going to do the shopping.*
Je *vais* acheter un ordinateur.	*I am going to buy a computer.*
Vous *allez* être malade, Kate?	*Are you going to be ill, Kate?*

2 *Le, la, les:* him, her, it, them

Imagine you are talking about people or things, let's say about somebody or something you know and must see – Pierre, Louise, a shop, the TV or the photos. If you want to say: *him*, *her*, *it* or *them*, in French you use: **le**, **la** or **les**. There is no special word for *it*.

Pierre?	**Je *le* connais, je dois *le* voir.**
Pierre?	*I know him, I must see him.*
Louise?	**Je *la* connais, je dois *la* voir.**
Louise?	*I know her, I must see her.*
Le magasin?	**Je *le* connais, je dois *le* voir.**
The shop?	*I know it, I must see it.*
La télé?	**Je *la* connais, je dois *la* voir.**
The television?	*I know it, I must see it.*
Les photos?	**Je *les* connais, je dois *les* voir.**
The photos?	*I know them, I must see them.*

Notice that **le**, **la** and **les** go right in front of the verb, if there is just one verb:

Je *le* connais.	*I him know.*

If there are two verbs **le**, **la** or **les** go in front of the second one:

Je dois *le* voir.	*I must him see.*

But in the past tense, **le**, **la**, **les** goes in front of the first verb:

Je *l'a* vu.	*I have seen him/her/it.*

3 Vous désirez? Je voudrais… *would like*

When eating out, the waiter or your host would normally ask: **Qu'est-ce que vous désirez?** And you would answer: **Je voudrais…**

(Not the other way around: **Vous voudriez? Je désire… Non, non!**)

Last two verb boxes: learn them now.

vouloir – *want (to)*	
je voudrais	*I would like (to)*
vous voudriez	*you would like (to)*
nous voudrions	*we would like (to)*
il/elle voudrait	*he/she would like (to)*
ils/elles voudraient	*they would like (to)*

pouvoir – *can*	
je peux	*I can*
but: puis-je?	*can I?*
vous pouvez	*you can*
nous pouvons	*we can*
il/elle peut	*he/she can*
ils/elles peuvent	*they can*

Learn by heart

🔊 CD2, tr 8

Pretend this is a telephone call by a rather opinionated person. When you have learned it by heart, try to act it out in 50 seconds.

Je suis très intéressant

Voudriez-vous dîner avec moi ce soir?
Je connais un très bon restaurant et le vin est superbe.
Non?
Pourquoi pas? Je suis très intéressant.
Vous ne me connaissez pas?
Mais bien sûr. Vous me voyez beaucoup à la télé.
La météo* – c'est moi (*French weather forecast***)**
Vous ne pouvez pas? Pourquoi pas?
Vous avez un rendez-vous important?
Oh, non! Ce n'est pas possible!

If you are short of time this week, you can settle for the slightly shorter piece which follows… or you could do both!

Je ne l'aime pas

Vous connaissez Monsieur Dupont? Je dois aller dîner avec lui.
Pourquoi?
C'est un très bon client du bureau. Mais je ne l'aime pas. Il mange et il boit trop.
Et quand?
Ce soir! Il y a du football à la télé! Toujours le bureau!
Ah, je suis désolée!

This week's tip: *vous* or *tu*?

There are two ways of saying *you* in French: **vous** or **tu**. **Vous** is formal and polite. When you are in France and speak French use **vous**. **Tu** is for family and friends, and needs a whole lot of extra grammar. Next year, perhaps.

Say it simply

When people want to speak French but don't dare, it's usually because they are trying to *translate* what they want to say from English into French. But because they don't know some of the words, they give up.

With **Traveller's French**, you work around the words you don't know with the words you know. And believe me, 389 words are enough to say almost anything. It may not always be very elegant – but that's not the point. You are speaking, *communicating*.

Here are three examples showing you how to say things in a simple way. I have highlighted the English words which are not part of the vocabulary.

1 In English:

You need to **change** your **flight** to London from Tuesday to Friday.

Saying it simply:

Nous ne pouvons pas aller à Londres mardi, nous voudrions aller à Londres vendredi.

We cannot go to London Tuesday, we would like to go to London Friday.

or: **Mardi n'est pas bon pour nous. Nous voudrions prendre l'avion vendredi.**

Tuesday is not good for us. We would like to take the plane Friday.

2 In English:

You want to get your **purse** from the coach, which the driver has locked.

Saying it simply:

J'ai besoin de mon argent. Il est dans le bus mais le bus n'est pas ouvert.

I need my money. It is in the bus but the bus is not open.

3 This time your friend has just cracked the heel of her only pair of shoes. You have to catch a train soon and need some help. This is what you could say simply:

Excusez-moi, nous avons un problème avec une chaussure. Il y a un magasin par ici où on peut la réparer – maintenant?

Excuse me, we have a problem with a shoe. Is there a shop around here where one can repair it – now?

Let's speak French

CD2, tr 9

Here are ten sentences as a warm-up. Listen to the recording if you have it.

1 Who has telephoned and why?
2 He says that I know him.
3 I believe that we have (the) time later.
4 I do not like the chicken.
5 A glass of red wine, please.
6 Yes, sure, I have (an) appointment with you.
7 Everybody is on holiday.
8 He said that it is all right.
9 I can go next week with him.
10 Does somebody have the number?

Now pretend you are in France with friends who do not speak French. They want you to ask someone things in French. They say: *Please ask him…*

11 if he can help the client
12 if he phoned yesterday
13 why he has bought the Ferrari
14 if he has (an) appointment today
15 where one can buy a newspaper

On another occasion your friends will ask you to **tell** someone things. If you don't know the odd word work round it by using the ones you do. Tell them…

16 that the soup is stone cold
17 that she is a vegetarian
18 that we don't have his number
19 that we are unfortunately in a rush now
20 that next week will suit us

Answers

1 Qui a téléphoné et pourquoi?
2 Il dit que je le connais.
3 Je crois que nous avons le temps plus tard.
4 Je n'aime pas le poulet.
5 Un verre de vin rouge, s'il vous plaît.
6 Oui, bien sûr, j'ai un rendez-vous avec vous.
7 Tout le monde est en vacances.
8 Il a dit que c'est bien.
9 Je peux aller avec lui la semaine prochaine.
10 Quelqu'un a le numéro?
11 Vous pouvez aider le client?
12 Vous avez téléphoné hier?
13 Pourquoi avez-vous acheté la Ferrari?
14 Vous avez rendez-vous aujourd'hui?
15 Où peut-on acheter un journal?
16 Excusez-moi mais la soupe est froide.
17 Elle ne mange pas de viande.
18 Nous n'avons pas son numéro.
19 Malheureusement nous n'avons pas le temps maintenant.
20 C'est bien, la semaine prochaine.

Let's speak more French

🔊 CD2, tr 10

In your own words

This exercise will teach you to express yourself freely. Use only the words you have learned so far.

Tell me in your own words that...

1 somebody telephoned – you think it was Georges Leclair
2 you have (an) appointment with him next week
3 he works for the bank
4 he is a very good client
5 you worked with Georges on Saturday
6 Edith Palmer cannot eat with us – she is ill
7 she doesn't have much time to go (*pour aller*) to the doctor
8 you would like to help her (her to help), but you don't have her telephone number
9 we were at the restaurant at half past eleven
10 everyone liked the escalopes and the chocolate mousse

Answers

1 Quelqu'un a téléphoné – je crois que c'était Georges Leclair.
2 J'ai rendez-vous avec lui la semaine prochaine.
3 Il travaille pour la banque.
4 C'est un très bon client.
5 J'ai travaillé avec Georges samedi.
6 Edith Palmer ne peut pas dîner avec nous – elle est malade.
7 Elle n'a pas beaucoup de temps pour aller chez le médecin.
8 Je voudrais l'aider, mais je n'ai pas son numéro de téléphone.
9 Nous étions au restaurant à onze heures et demie.
10 Tout le monde a aimé les escalopes et la mousse au chocolat.

Let's speak French – fast and fluently

🔊 CD2, tr 11

Translate each section into English and check if it is correct. Then cover up the answers and say the three or four sentences as quickly and correctly as you can.

If you manage to say each paragraph in less than 25 seconds you are doing very well.

Some of the English is in 'French-speak' to help you.

Do you know Georges Leclair? He phoned yesterday.
Why? He said it was important.
The appointment in Paris was on Wednesday.

Vous connaissez Georges Leclair? Il a téléphoné hier.
Pourquoi? Il a dit que c'était important.
Le rendez-vous à Paris était mercredi.

Georges is in Toulouse until Friday.
There is an excellent restaurant in front of the bank.
I would like to eat with him tonight.

Georges est à Toulouse jusqu'à vendredi.
Il y a un restaurant superbe devant la banque.
Je voudrais dîner avec lui ce soir.

Unfortunately, I cannot eat with him.
My dog is ill. He has eaten too much meat.
Oh, I am very sorry. How do you say in French: 'Poor little thing?'
(le pauvre)

Malheureusement, je ne peux pas dîner avec lui.
Mon chien est malade. Il a mangé trop de viande.
Oh, je suis désolé(e). Comment dit-on en français: 'Poor little thing'? 'Le pauvre'.

Spot the keys

CD2, tr 12

You practised listening for key words when you asked the way to the post office in Week 3. Now you are in a department store and ask the sales assistant if the black shoes you fancy are also available in size 39. She says **non,** then **un moment, s'il vous plaît** and disappears. When she comes back this is what she says:

J'ai téléphoné ànotrecentrale mais illeurreste ce modèle de **chaussures seulement** *en* **bleu**. *Maisnousenavonsen* **noir** *en* **trente-huit** *et je sais par expérience que ce modèle chausse normalement* **très grand.** *Àmonavis elles seront* **assez grandes.**

Size 39 was only available in blue but size 38 might be big enough.

Test your progress

Translate into French:

1 Sure, the appointment was Wednesday, at the bank.
2 Next week? No, that's not possible. We don't have (the) time.
3 I would like a glass of champagne and then a bottle of white wine.
4 Can you help me, please? Someone needs the number of the doctor.
5 He said that the town centre is very interesting. Have you seen it?
6 We would like to eat with you Monday evening.
7 Where can one buy fruit and vegetables around here?
8 The cashpoint machine is upstairs, in front of the exit.
9 We'll take the chicken or the ham salad. The fish is too expensive.
10 I know the wines of Bordeaux well. They are superb.
11 On Friday we are going to the client. It is a very important matter.
12 I would like to buy something. How do you say in French…?
13 I do not like the Mercedes. I am going to take the small Peugeot.
14 He says that he has the flu and that he has not finished the work.
15 Everybody has phoned this evening. It's crazy.
16 Who saw that the dog has eaten my meat?
17 There is ice cream. But I do not like chocolate ice cream.
18 How are you? You are sick? You must drink a lot of water.
19 When are we going to Lyon and why?
20 What are we doing in this hotel? It is horrible.

If you are happy with your result take it straight to the **Progress Chart.**

Week 5

Day-by-day guide

How about 15 minutes on the train, tube or bus, 10 minutes on the way home and 20 minutes before switching on the television?

Day one

- Read **On the move**.
- Listen to/Read **En route**.
- Read the New words. Learn 15 or more.

Day two

- Repeat **En route** and the **New words**.
- Cut out the **Flash words** and get stuck in.

Day three

- Test yourself to perfection on all the **New words**.
- Listen to/Read **Learn by heart**.

Day four

- Cut out and learn the **Flash sentences**.
- Read and learn the **Good news grammar**.

Day five

- Listen to/Read **Let's speak French**.

Day six

- Listen to/Read **Let's speak more French** (optional).
- Listen to/Read **Let's speak French – fast and fluently** (optional).
- Listen to/Read **Spot the keys**.
- Translate **Test your progress**.

Day seven

How is the **Progress chart** looking? Great? Great! I bet you don't want a day off… but I insist.

On the move

Tom and Kate are off on their travels again – by train, bus and hire car.

(At the station)

Tom Two tickets to Cannes, please.

Clerk Return tickets?

Tom What? Can you speak more slowly, please?

Clerk Return... tickets?

Tom One way, please. At what time does the train leave, and from where?

Clerk At nine forty-five, platform eight.

Kate Tom, quickly, here are two non-smoking seats.* Oh, somebody is smoking over there. Excuse me, it is forbidden to smoke because it is non-smoking here.

Man Sorry, I don't understand, I come from England.

(At the bus stop)

Kate The next bus for Nice is at six o'clock. We have to wait ten minutes. Tom, here are my postcards and a letter. There is a letterbox down below. I am going to take some photos over there. The coast is superb in the sun.

Tom Kate, quickly, here are two blue buses. This one is full. Let's take the other one. (*In the bus*) Two tickets for Nice, please.

Driver This bus goes only to Cannes.

Tom But we are in Cannes.

Driver Yes, yes, but the bus goes to the Cannes hospital.

(In the car)

Tom Here is our car. Only €70 for three days. I am very pleased.

Kate I do not like this car. It was not expensive because it is old. I hope that we are not going to have a problem.

Tom I am sorry, but the first car was too expensive and the second one too big. This one was the last. (*Later*) Where are we? Where is the map? On the left there is a service station and on the right a school. Quickly!

*Smoking is no longer permitted in any compartment on French trains.

En route

🔊 CD2, tr 13

Tom and Kate are off on their travels again – by train, bus and hire car.

(À la gare)

Tom Deux billets pour Cannes, s'il vous plaît.

Clerk Aller-retour?

Tom Comment? Pouvez-vous parler plus lentement, s'il vous plaît?

Clerk Aller… retour?

Tom Aller simple, s'il vous plaît. À quelle heure part le train, et d'où?

Clerk À neuf heures quarante cinq, quai huit.

Kate Tom, vite, ici il y a deux places pour non-fumeurs.* Oh, quelqu'un fume là-bas. Excusez-moi, c'est interdit de fumer parce que c'est non-fumeur ici.

Man Sorry, je ne comprends pas. Je viens from England.

(À l'arrêt de bus)

Kate Le prochain bus pour Nice est à six heures. Nous devons attendre dix minutes. Tom, voilà mes cartes postales et une lettre. Il y a une boîte aux lettres en bas. Je vais prendre des photos là-bas. La côte est superbe au soleil.

Tom Kate, vite, voilà deux bus bleus. Celui-ci est plein. Prenons l'autre. (*Dans le bus*) Deux billets pour Nice, s'il vous plaît.

Driver Ce bus va seulement à Cannes.

Tom Mais nous sommes à Cannes.

Driver Oui, oui, mais le bus va jusqu'à l'hôpital de Cannes.

(Dans la voiture)

Tom Voilà notre voiture. Seulement soixante-dix euros pour trois jours. Je suis très content.

Kate Je n'aime pas cette voiture. Elle n'était pas chère parce qu'elle est vieille. J'espère que nous n'allons pas avoir de problème.

Tom Je suis désolé, mais la première voiture était trop chère et la deuxième trop grande. Celle-ci était la dernière. (*Plus tard*) Où sommes-nous? Où est la carte? À gauche, il y a une station-service et à droite, une école. Vite!

Kate We are coming from the underground station. The main road is over there, next to the traffic light. If we go to the end, we are on the motorway. In three kilometres. (*On the motorway*) Why is this car so slow? Do we have enough petrol? How many litres? Do we have enough oil? Is the engine too hot? I believe the car has broken down. Where is the mobile? Where is the number of the garage? Where is my bag?

Tom My God, Kate! All these questions! Here comes the rain! And why are the police behind us?

Kate Nous venons de la station de métro. La rue principale est là-bas, à côté du feu rouge. Si nous allons jusqu'au bout, nous sommes sur l'autoroute. À trois kilomètres. (*Sur l'autoroute*) Pourquoi cette voiture est-elle si lente? Avons-nous assez d'essence? Combien de litres? Avons-nous assez d'huile? Le moteur est trop chaud? Je crois que la voiture est en panne. Où est le téléphone portable? Où est le numéro du garage? Où est mon sac?

Tom Mon Dieu, Kate! Toutes ces questions! Voilà la pluie! Et pourquoi la police est-elle derrière nous?

New words

CD2, tr 14

en route on the move
la gare the railway station
le billet the ticket
aller-retour return ticket, *lit.* go-return
comment how, what, pardon?
parler/parlé to speak/spoken
lente, lentement slow, slowly
aller simple one way (ticket)
il part he, it leaves
le train the train
le quai the platform
vite quick, quickly
non-fumeur non-smoking
il fume he smokes
là-bas over there
interdit forbidden
fumer/fumé to smoke/smoked
parce que because
je ne comprends pas I do not understand
je viens I come
l'arrêt (de bus) the (bus) stop
attendre/attendu to wait/waited
voilà here is, there is
la carte postale the postcard
la lettre the letter
la boîte the box
en bas down below
la photo the photo
la côte the coast
le soleil the sun
celui-ci, celle-ci this one
plein(e) full
l'hôpital the hospital
la voiture the car
notre our
content(e) pleased
vieux, vieille old
j'espère/espéré I hope/hoped
le premier, la première the first
le/la deuxième the second
le dernier, la dernière the last
la carte the map
la station-service the petrol station
l'école the school
nous venons we come, are coming
la station metro stop, station (bus)
le métro the metro (underground)
la rue principale the main road
à côté de next to, at the side of
le feu rouge the traffic light
si if, so
le bout the end
l'autoroute the motorway
l'essence the petrol
le litre the litre
l'huile the oil
le moteur the engine
chaud(e) hot
le garage the garage, workshop
la pluie the rain
la police the police

TOTAL NEW WORDS: 61
... Only 32 words to go!

Learn by heart

CD2, tr 15

Someone has crashed the car and someone else is getting suspicious! Try to say these lines fluently and like a prize-winning play.

Pouvons-nous aller au tennis?

Pouvons-nous aller au tennis?
Quelqu'un du bureau m'a donné deux billets.
Je voudrais voir le match des Américains.
Nous pouvons prendre le bus, le métro ou le train.

Le bus? le métro? le train? Pourquoi?
Qu'est-ce qu'il y a?
Nous avons une bonne voiture en bas.

Alors... il y avait de la pluie et je n'ai pas vu le feu rouge,
mais ce n'est rien...
et le garçon du garage était très sympathique!

Good news grammar

🔊 CD2, tr 16

1 How to say: 'my', 'your', 'our', 'his', 'her', 'their'...

...winning lottery ticket, or anything else that belongs to someone.

Here's a box of tricks worth more than just a fleeting glance. You will use these 12 words every day, and they are quite easy to remember. You have met them before. Take three minutes to revise them.

mon, ma, mes	votre, vos	notre, nos	son, sa, ses	leur, leurs
my	*your*	*our*	*his, her*	*their*

Imagine you want to say: *my newspaper*, *my car* or *my shoes*. As you can see, there are three choices. So which one to pick? It's **mon journal, ma voiture** and **mes chaussures.**

Can you see what happened? **mon** goes with **le** words, **ma** goes with **la** words and **mes** goes with **les** words.

Notre and **votre** and **leur** are easy: **notre église** *our church*, **votre école** *your school*, **leur maison** *their house*. Use **nos, vos,** and **leurs** for more than one thing, all words that start with **les: nos vacances** *our holidays*, **vos parents** *your parents*, **leurs enfants** *their children*.

But what about **son travail**? Does this mean *his* or *her work*? Both! The same applies to **sa mère,** *his* or *her mother*, and **ses amis,** *his* or *her friends*. If you get in a muddle and say **son mère** and **sa travail? Pas de problème!** Amazingly people will understand you.

2 Me, you, us, him, her, them

Is this winning lottery ticket, pay increase, boring book... for *me*, *you* or *him*? Here's another revision box. Have a two-minute look.

pour...	moi	vous	nous	lui	elle	eux	elles
for...	*me*	*you*	*us*	*him*	*her*	*them (m.)*	*them (f.)*

These words also work with **avec, sans, de, chez, devant** and **derrière.**

For example, **avec nous** *with us*, **sans moi** *without me*, **chez vous** *at your place/house*, **devant lui** *in front of him*.

Let's speak French

🔊 CD2, tr 17

Here's your ten-point warm up: I'll give you an answer and you ask me a question – as if you did not hear very clearly the words in CAPITALS.

Example: Pierre est ICI. Question: Où est Pierre?

1 Le téléphone portable est DANS MON SAC.
2 L'AUTOROUTE est là-bas.
3 Le bus part DANS VINGT MINUTES.
4 TOM voudrait parler avec Monsieur Durant.
5 Un aller-retour pour Paris, c'est 42 EUROS.
6 Je n'aime pas la maison PARCE QU'elle est très vieille.
7 Ils vont en Angleterre EN VOITURE.
8 Je n'ai pas vu LE FEU ROUGE.
9 NON, je n'aime pas le garage.
10 OUI, je suis content de l'école.

Now answer starting with **oui** and **nous**:

11 Vous avez la carte de l'autoroute?
12 Vous allez prendre ce bus?
13 Vous pouvez fumer dans le train?
14 Vous devez attendre vingt minutes?
15 Vous allez maintenant à la gare?
16 Vous aimez la côte?

Explain these words in French:

17 kennels **18** teacher **19** unemployed **20** to be broke

Answers

1 Où est le téléphone portable?
2 C'est quoi, là-bas?
3 Quand part le bus?
4 Qui voudrait parler avec Monsieur Durant?
5 C'est combien un aller-retour pour Paris?
6 Pourquoi vous n'aimez pas la maison?
7 Comment vont-ils en Angleterre?
8 Qu'est-ce que vous n'avez pas vu?
9 Vous n'aimez pas le garage?
10 Êtes-vous content de l'école?
11 Oui, nous avons la carte de l'autoroute.
12 Oui, nous allons prendre ce bus.
13 Oui, nous pouvons fumer dans le train.
14 Oui, nous devons attendre vingt minutes.
15 Oui, nous allons maintenant à la gare.
16 Oui, nous aimons la côte.
17 Une maison pour les chiens quand nous sommes en vacances.
18 Le monsieur ou la dame qui travaille avec les enfants à l'école.
19 Quelqu'un qui ne travaille pas.
20 Nous n'avons pas d'argent. Pas un euro!

Let's speak more French

🔊 CD2, tr 18

In your own words

This exercise will teach you to express yourself freely. Use only the words you have learned so far.

Tell me in your own words that...

1 you bought a return ticket for Marseille
2 there is a train at 10.15
3 it is forbidden, but somebody is smoking in a non-smoking seat
4 on Monday you wouldn't mind going by (*en*) bus to Narbonne
5 you must take some photos for your mother
6 this bus is crowded; you are going to take the other one
7 your car is old and very cheap
8 your wife says: 'It's terrible, I don't like it'
9 she says the car is too slow and the engine overheats
10 hopefully you won't have a problem

Answers

1 J'ai acheté un billet aller-retour pour Marseille.
2 Il y a un train à dix heures et quart.
3 C'est interdit, mais quelqu'un fume dans une place non-fumeur.
4 Je voudrais aller lundi à Narbonne en bus.
5 Je dois prendre des photos pour ma mère.
6 Ce bus est plein. Je vais prendre l'autre.
7 Ma voiture est vieille et très bon marché.
8 Ma femme dit: 'C'est terrible, je ne l'aime pas.'
9 Elle dit que la voiture est trop lente et que le moteur est trop chaud.
10 J'espère que nous n'allons pas avoir de problème.

Let's speak French – fast and fluently

CD2, tr 19

Translate each section and check if it is correct, then cover up the answers and say the three or four sentences as quickly and correctly as you can. Try to say each section in less than 25 seconds.

Some of the English is in 'French-speak' to help you.

A ticket for Lille, please, only one way.
How much? €71? Can you speak more slowly, please?
Thank you. When does the train leave?

Un billet pour Lille, s'il vous plaît, aller simple.
Combien? Soixante et onze euros? Pouvez-vous parler plus lentement, s'il vous plaît?
Merci. À quelle heure part le train?

My husband is going to take a photo of the post box.
Here the post boxes are not red.
Unfortunately, it (she) is full.
What are we going to do with the letters?

Mon mari va prendre une photo de la boîte aux lettres.
Ici les boîtes aux lettres ne sont pas rouges.
Malheureusement elle est pleine.
Qu'est-ce que nous allons faire avec les lettres?

We don't have (a) map of the Alps.
I can't see the motorway.
My friend is ill with a headache (pains of head).
We have a problem. Our car is broken.

Nous n'avons pas de carte des Alpes.
Je ne peux pas voir l'autoroute.
Mon ami est malade avec des maux de tête.
Nous avons un problème. Notre voiture est en panne.

Now say all the sentences in French without stopping and starting. If you can do it in under one minute you are a fast and fluent winner! But if you are not happy with your result – just try once more.

Spot the keys

🔊 CD2, tr 20

This time you're planning a trip in the country. What about the weather? This is what you ask:

Excusez-moi, quel temps fait-il aujourd'hui?

Here's the answer:

> *Eh bien,* **je ne suis pas sûr si** *le dernier bulletin* **météo à la télévision est correct,** *mais d'après eux le système de basse pression se déplace progressivement et ils disent qu'il fera encore* **chaud aujourd'hui,** *environ* **vingt-cinq** *degrés. Mais nous aurons probablement encore* **un peu de pluie ce soir.**

He doesn't seem to be sure. According to the TV, it will be warm today – 25°C – with a little rain in the evening.

Test your progress

Translate the following into French and write down your answers.

1 At what time is the next bus?
2 How much does a return ticket cost?
3 What did you say? Can you speak more slowly, please?
4 I do not understand why petrol is cheaper (less expensive) in America.
5 It is forbidden to smoke in the underground.
6 Quickly, here is the train. Platform three.
7 This box is for (the) postcards? A yellow letterbox?
8 Hello, I am coming from Calais. Is that the garage?
9 I hope that this is not the last service station.
10 It is very hot this week. I would like a little rain.
11 She did not wait for the traffic light. Now she is in hospital.
12 We did not see much sun. I am not happy.
13 She talks and smokes too much on the motorway! I am going to take the train.
14 We are at the police (station) because somebody has taken our mobile phone.
15 The tickets are cheap if you buy them now.
16 I like your Ferrari. Was it (she) very expensive?
17 There is a chemist's behind the main road, next to the bus stop.
18 How is the car? It is old but the engine is new.
19 I need two tickets. Are there non-smoking seats?
20 Excuse me, I do not know the town. Where is the station?

If you know all your words, you should score over 90%!

Week 6

Day-by-day guide

This is your last week! Need I say more?

Day one

- Read **At the airport.**
- Listen to/Read **À l'aéroport.**
- Read the **New words.** There are only 32.

Day two

- Repeat **À l'aéroport** and learn all the **New words.**
- Work with the **Flash words** and **Flash sentences.**

Day three

- Test yourself on the **Flash sentences.**
- Listen to/Read **Learn by heart.**

Day four

- No more **Good news grammar**. Have a look at the summary.
- Read **Say it simply.**
- Listen to/Read **Spot the keys.**

Day five

- Listen to/Read **Let's speak French.**

Day six

- Listen to/Read **Let's speak more French** (optional).
- Listen to/Read **Let's speak French – fast and fluently** (optional).
- Your last **Test your progress**. Go for it!

Day seven

Congratulations!
You have successfully completed the course
and can now speak
Traveller's French

At the airport

It's the end of the trip and time to go home. There's one more surprise for Tom and Kate when they bump into an old friend in the departure lounge.

Tom We have to work on Monday. It's horrible! I would like to leave for Italy now, or take a plane for Hawaii. The office can wait. Nobody ever knows where I am.

Kate And what are the people in my office going to say? They wait two days and telephone my mother. She'll surely give them the number of my mobile. And then?

Tom Yes, yes, I know. Well, perhaps a week at Christmas in the snow or on a boat in Portugal... I'm going to buy a newspaper... Kate. Here is Mr Cardin.

Henri Hello, how are you? What are you doing here? Here is my wife, Nancy. Your holidays are over? Were they good?

Kate Provence was wonderful. We have seen a lot of things and have eaten much too much. We know the Côte d'Azur well now.

Henri Well, next year the Loire? Or you must come to Toulouse. Mrs Walker, my wife would like to buy a book on computers. Can you go with her and help her? Mr Walker, can you give me the newspaper? Is there something about the football? We have a beer afterwards?

(At the airport kiosk)

Kate I don't see anything here. And what I see I do not like. Are you also going to England?

Nancy No, we are going to Bordeaux to Henri's mother. She often has our children during the holidays. A boy and three girls. We are going to take the train tomorrow. It is less expensive.

Kate Your husband works for the Bank of France?

Nancy Yes, his work is interesting but not very well paid. We have a small apartment and an old Citroën. There is a lot to repair. My parents are in Los Angeles and I have a girlfriend in Dallas. We write a lot of e-mails. I would like to go to Los Angeles or Dallas but it is too expensive.

Kate But you have a beautiful house in St Tropez.

À l'aéroport

🔊 CD2, tr 21

It's the end of the trip and time to go home. There's one more surprise for Tom and Kate when they bump into an old friend in the departure lounge.

Tom Nous devons travailler lundi. C'est horrible! Je voudrais partir en Italie maintenant ou prendre l'avion pour Hawaii. Le bureau peut attendre. Personne ne sait jamais où je suis.

Kate Et que disent les gens dans mon bureau? Ils attendent deux jours et téléphonent à ma mère. Elle leur donne bien sûr le numéro de mon portable. Et après?

Tom Oui, oui, je sais. Alors, peut-être une semaine à Noël à la neige ou sur un bateau au Portugal... Je vais acheter le journal... Kate. Voici Monsieur Cardin.

Henri Bonjour, ça va? Que faites-vous ici? Voici ma femme, Nancy. Vos vacances sont terminées? C'étaient bien?

Kate La Provence était merveilleuse. Nous avons vu beaucoup de choses et beaucoup trop mangé. Nous connaissons bien la Côte d'Azur maintenant.

Henri L'année prochaine, la Loire, alors? Ou vous devez venir à Toulouse. Madame Walker, ma femme voudrait acheter un livre sur les ordinateurs. Pouvez-vous aller avec elle et l'aider? Monsieur Walker, pouvez-vous me donner le journal? Il y a quelque chose sur le football? Nous prenons une bière après?

(Au kiosque de l'aéroport)

Kate Je ne vois rien ici. Et ce que je vois, je n'aime pas. Vous allez aussi en Angleterre?

Nancy Non, nous allons à Bordeaux, chez la mère de Henri. Elle a souvent nos enfants pendant les vacances. Un garçon et trois filles. Nous prenons le train demain. Ça coûte moins cher.

Kate Votre mari travaille à la Banque de France?

Nancy Oui, son travail est intéressant mais pas très bien payé. Nous avons un petit appartement et une vieille Citroën. Il y a beaucoup à réparer. Mes parents sont à Los Angeles et j'ai une amie à Dallas. Nous nous écrivons beaucoup de courriels. Je voudrais aller à Los Angeles ou Dallas mais ça coûte trop cher.

Kate Mais vous avez une belle maison à St Tropez.

Nancy A house in St Tropez? I do not know the Côte d'Azur. When we have holidays we go to Lille to friends.

Tom Kate, quickly. We have a plane to catch. Goodbye. What is the matter, Kate? What did Mrs Cardin say?

Kate Wait, Tom, wait!

New words

🔊 CD2, tr 22

l'aéroport the airport
partir to leave
il sait he knows (a fact)
jamais never, ever
ils disent/dit they say/said
les gens the people
ils attendent/attendu they wait/ waited
ils téléphonent they phone
la mère the mother
leur them
elle donne she gives
je sais I know (a fact)
à Noël at Christmas
à la neige in the snow
un bateau a boat
voici here is
merveilleux (-euse) wonderful
nous connaissons we know
l'année the (course of the) year
le livre the book
venir to come
donner/donné to give/given
je vois/vu I see/seen
souvent often
pendant during
le garçon the boy
la fille the girl
l'appartement the apartment
nous écrivons/écrit we write/ written
le courriel e-mail
chez des amis at/to friends
attendez! wait!

TOTAL NEW WORDS: 32
Total French words learned: 389
Extra words: 77
GRAND TOTAL: 466

Nancy Une maison à St Tropez? Je ne connais pas la Côte d'Azur. Quand nous avons des vacances, nous allons à Lille chez des amis.

Tom Kate, vite. Nous avons un avion à prendre. Au revoir. Qu'est-ce qu'il y a, Kate? Qu'est-ce que Madame Cardin a dit?

Kate Attendez, Tom, attendez!

Learn by heart

CD2, tr 23

This is your last dialogue to learn by heart. Give it your best. You now have a large store of everyday phrases which will be very useful.

Au revoir...

Kate	**Bonjour, Monsieur Durant, c'est Kate Walker, de l'aéroport Charles de Gaulle. Oui, malheureusement nos vacances sont terminées. Merci beaucoup pour mardi soir. Tom voudrait parler avec vous... au revoir.**
Tom	**Allô, Alain! Quoi? Vous allez acheter les deux? Mon bureau a votre courriel? C'est merveilleux. Merci beaucoup. L'année prochaine? Je voudrais voir la Loire. Avec Edith Palmer? Mon Dieu, non, non! Nous devons prendre l'avion. Au revoir.**

Tip of the week

Plus and *moins*

If you want to say that something is *bigger*, *hotter* or *more beautiful* you just add **plus**:

***plus* grand(e), *plus* chaud(e), *plus* beau/belle**

If you want to say that something is *less expensive* or *less interesting*, you use **moins**:

***moins* cher/chère, *moins* intéressant(e)**

Good news grammar

As promised, there is no new grammar in this lesson. However, at times you may get entangled in the various verb forms, so here is a summary of all the verbs which appear in the six weeks. When you read through them, you'll realize how many you know!

VERB	JE	VOUS	NOUS	IL/ELLE	ILS/ELLES	THE PAST
acheter						acheté
aider						aidé
aimer	aime	aimez	aimons	aime	aiment	aimé
aller	vais	allez	allons	va	vont	
attendre		attendez		attend	attendent	attendu
avoir	ai	avez	avons	a	ont	
	avais		avions	avait	avaient	
boire	bois		buvons	boit		
désirer		désirez				
devoir	dois	devez	devons	doit	doivent	
dîner						dîné
dire				dit	disent	dit
donner				donne		donné
connaître	connais	connaissez	connaissons	connaît	connaissent	connu
croire	crois	croyez	croyons	croit	croient	
écrire			écrivons	écrit		écrit
espérer	espère		espérons			espéré
être	suis	êtes	sommes	est	sont	
	étais	étiez	étions	était	étaient	
faire	fais	faites	faisons	fait	font	fait
fumer	fume	fumez	fumons	fume	fument	fumé
manger	mange	mangez	mangeons	mange	mangent	mangé
parler	parle	parlez	parlons	parle	parlent	parlé
partir	pars	partez	partons	part	partent	
pouvoir	peux	pouvez	pouvons	peut	peuvent	
prendre	prends	prenez	prenons	prend	prennent	pris
réparer						réparé
savoir	sais	savez	savons	sait	savent	
téléphoner					téléphonent	téléphoné
travailler	travaille	travaillez	travaillons	travaille	travaillent	travaillé
venir	viens	venez	venons	vient	viennent	
voir	vois	voyez	voyons	voit	voient	vu
vouloir	voudrais	voudriez	voudrions	voudrait	voudraient	

You'll notice lots of gaps. These are the ones I don't think you need to bother with for now. If you are dead keen, you can always look them up in a French grammar book.

Tip: To say *I went to*, use *I was in*: **J'étais à Paris.** *I was in Paris.*

Say it simply

1 You are asking the dry cleaner for a same-day service since you are leaving tomorrow. You also explain that the stain may be red wine.
2 You are at the airport, about to catch your flight home, when you realize that you have left some clothes behind in the room of your hotel. You phone the hotel to ask the housekeeper to send the things on to you.

What would you say? Say it, then write it down. Then take a look at our examples in the **Answers** section.

Spot the keys

🔊 CD2, tr 24

Here are two final practice rounds. If you have the recording, close the book now. Find the key words and try to get the gist of it. Then look at the translation in the **Answers** section.

You might ask a taxi driver:

Combien de temps pour aller à l'aéroport? Et c'est combien?

His answer:

Cela dépend quand vous y allez. Normalement, ça prend vingt minutes mais s'il y a beaucoup de circulation et le pont sur la rivière est bouché, ça prend trois quarts d'heure. Le prix est celui que marque le compteur. Normalement, c'est quarante, cinquante euros environ.

While killing time in the departure lounge of the airport, you could not help overhearing someone who seems to be raving about something. Identify the key words and guess where they have been.

... et les gens sont vraiment très gentils et pas aussi réservés qu'on le dit. L'hôtel était sur la plage et vu le temps merveilleux, nous avons fait beaucoup d'excursions dans la campagne qui est très belle et visité un tas d'endroits intéressants. Et le dîner à l'hôtel, vraiment très bon – rien à redire et pas cher. C'est pourquoi nous avons décidé tout de suite: l'année prochaine nous reviendrons sûrement en...

Let's speak French

🔊 CD2, tr 25

A five point warm-up. Answer these questions using the words in brackets.

1 Il a acheté l'appartement à Marbella? (Oui, lundi)
2 Vous voudriez partir en Italie? (Oui, mardi)
3 Il sait que vous venez? (Oui, ce soir)
4 Pourquoi réparez-vous toujours votre voiture? (parce que, vieille)
5 Il a pris le train d'abord? (non, le métro)

In the next exercise you are going to act as an interpreter again, this time telling your French friend in French what others have said in English (the bit in brackets). Each time say the whole sentence out loud.

6 Quelqu'un dit que vous êtes fou *(if you buy this house).*
7 Quelqu'un dit qu'il n'aime pas ça *(if you come late*).
8 Quelqu'un dit que la douche est en panne *(if you don't have hot water).*
9 Mon ami a dit *(that our holidays are over).*
10 Elle a dit aussi *(that we are going to France next Christmas).*
11 Ma femme voudrait dire *(that she has flu)...*
12 et qu'elle ne peut pas aller en France *(because she is often ill).*
13 Mes parents ne peuvent pas aller en vacances *(because they are old).*
14 Mon ami dit *(that she is very beautiful).*
15 Il dit aussi *(that he would like her number).*

Answers

1 Oui, il a acheté l'appartement lundi.
2 Oui, je voudrais/nous voudrions partir mardi.
3 Oui, il sait que je viens/nous venons ce soir.
4 Je la répare toujours parce qu'elle est vieille.
5 Non, d'abord il a pris le métro.
6 ... si vous achetez cette maison.
7 ... si vous venez tard.
8 ... si vous n'avez pas d'eau chaude.
9 ... que nos vacances sont terminées.
10 ... que nous allons en France à Noël prochain.
11 ... qu'elle a la grippe.
12 ... parce qu'elle est souvent malade.
13 ... parce qu'ils sont vieux.
14 ... qu'elle est très belle.
15 ... qu'il voudrait son numéro.

Let's speak more French

CD2, tr 26

In your own words

This exercise will teach you to express yourself freely. Use only the words you have learned so far.

Tell me in your own words that…

1 next week you have to work
2 you don't like to work; you'd rather have more leave
3 nobody knows that you are in Corsica (*Corse*)
4 your mother has the number of your mobile phone
5 your vacation in Burgundy (*Bourgogne*) was wonderful
6 you did a lot of sightseeing and ate too much
7 your friend Mr Leclair is on his way to (*en*) Avignon today
8 he is going to catch a train for Besançon tomorrow
9 your wife must go to Montreal because her father is ill
10 you would like to go to (*en*) Africa at Christmas, but by boat

---

Answers

1 **La semaine prochaine je dois travailler.**
2 **Je n'aime pas travailler. Je voudrais avoir plus de vacances.**
3 **Personne ne sait que je suis en Corse.**
4 **Ma mère a le numéro de mon portable.**
5 **Mes vacances en Bourgogne étaient superbes.**
6 **J'ai beaucoup vu et trop mangé.**
7 **Mon ami Monsieur Leclair va aujourd'hui en Avignon.**
8 **Il va prendre le train pour Besançon demain.**
9 **Ma femme doit aller à Montréal parce que son père est malade.**
10 **Je voudrais aller en Afrique à Noël, mais en bateau.**

Let's speak French – fast and fluently

🔊 CD2, tr 27

Translate each section and check if it is correct, then cover up the answers and say the three or four sentences as quickly and correctly as you can. If you manage to say each paragraph in less than 25 seconds you'll have become very fluent.

The people in my office work a lot.
We write many e-mails and talk to (with) the important clients.
They say that during the year they have bought too many books.

Les gens dans mon bureau travaillent beaucoup.
Nous écrivons beaucoup de courriels (d'e-mails) et parlons avec les clients importants.
Ils disent que pendant l'année ils ont acheté trop de livres.

I know the Pyrenees and the Alps very well.
Next year I would like to see the Côte d'Azur.
Would you like to come with me?

Je connais très bien les Pyrénées et les Alpes.
L'année prochaine je voudrais voir la Côte d'Azur.
Voulez-vous venir avec moi?

Hello, what are you doing here? What's the matter?
I need to repair my car and my flat. They are very old.
Can you help me (me help), please? I need 200 euros.

Bonjour, qu'est-ce que vous faites ici? Qu'est-ce qu'il y a?
Je dois réparer ma voiture et mon appartement. Ils sont très vieux.
Pouvez-vous m'aider, s'il vous plaît? J'ai besoin de deux cents euros.

Now say **all** the sentences in French without stopping and starting in under one minute. If you are not happy with your result – just try once more.

Test your progress

A lot has been included in this last test, including all 30 new verbs. But don't panic – it looks worse than it is. Go for it – you'll do brilliantly.

Translate into French, in writing:

1 We write a lot of e-mails because we have a computer.
2 How are you? What is the matter? Can I help you?
3 We are coming with a lot of people from the office.
4 He said that we are going to eat with friends.
5 During the Christmas holidays there is always a lot of snow.
6 The second case is in the bus. Can you take the black bag?
7 That's crazy: I believe that somebody has eaten my steak!
8 Why did you not telephone? We waited until yesterday.
9 Quickly! Have you seen a taxi? My plane is waiting.
10 I know (it). The airport is always open – day and night.
11 I have worked on a boat but the work was not well paid.
12 I would like to eat (dine) later. At half past eight. Is that all right?
13 Your mother is very nice and she makes wonderful cakes.
14 Have you taken a flat in London or on the coast?
15 We must work a lot of hours. Three boys and two girls at school – that's too much money.
16 I hope that the garage can repair it.
17 I know her. She always goes shopping with her dog.
18 Who said that it is forbidden to smoke here?
19 I would like to speak with the sales assistant, please. He gave me green shoes!
20 They say that you bought another Citroën.
21 What would you like to drink? We have a superb red wine.
22 Sunday and Monday the boat leaves at a quarter to six.
23 I am sorry, but **Traveller's French** is finished.

Check your answers then enter a final excellent score on the **Progress chart** and write out your **Certificate**.

Answers

How to score

From a total of 100%

- Subtract 1% for each wrong or missing word.
- Subtract 1% for the wrong form of the verb, e.g. **je sommes; nous suis.**
- Subtract 1% every time you mixed up the past, present and future.

There are no penalties for:

- wrong use of all those little words, like: **le, la,** etc. / **un, une** / **de, du,** etc. / **son, sa,** etc.
- wrong ending of adjectives like: **une maison bon.**
- wrong choice of words with similar meaning like: **à, en, dans, chez.**
- wrong verb form – as long as it sounds the same, like **je peut** instead of **je peux.**
- wrong or different word order.
- wrong spelling, missing accents, missing apostrophes, missing hyphens – as long as you say the word correctly.

100% MINUS YOUR PENALTIES WILL GIVE YOU YOUR WEEKLY SCORE.

Week 1: Test your progress

1 Bonjour, nous sommes Helen et Paul.
2 Je suis de Marseille. Vous aussi?
3 J'étais à Cannes en juillet.
4 Mes parents ont une Rover.
5 Nous allons à Nice avec la Renault et cinq enfants.
6 Je n'ai pas un bon poste.
7 J'ai besoin d'une maison pour les vacances.
8 Que faites-vous? Vous travaillez avec des ordinateurs?
9 Elle a deux postes et trois téléphones.
10 Excusez-moi, êtes-vous Madame Cardin?
11 Nous travaillons chez Renault. Le travail est bien payé.
12 Nous avons un ordinateur très cher.
13 Je suis en France, mais sans ma femme.
14 Nous étions sept mois à Paris. C'est beaucoup.
15 Je vais à Nice en avril. C'est une belle ville.

Your score: ______ %
Correct your answers, then read them out loud twice.

Week 2: Test your progress

1 Nous voudrions prendre un café.
2 Il y a une banque par ici?
3 Nous allons manger quelque chose.
4 Vous avez l'addition pour le thé, s'il vous plaît?
5 Mes enfants n'ont pas assez d'argent.
6 Où est la chambre?
7 Ils vont toujours au café à six heures et demie.
8 Une autre question, s'il vous plaît: où sont les toilettes, tout droit?
9 Vous allez à Oslo en janvier?
10 Elle va à Los Angeles avec son mari.
11 Le petit déjeuner est superbe. C'est combien?
12 Où êtes-vous demain à dix heures et demie?
13 Il y a une banque à gauche.
14 Je vais en vacances en juillet.
15 Excusez-moi, nous avons seulement une carte de crédit.
16 D'accord, nous prenons la Renault pour deux jours.
17 Nous allons réparer la Citroën. Elle est en panne.

18 Je travaille douze heures. Nous avons besoin d'argent.
19 Trois euros pour un thé froid? C'est trop!
20 Il y a quarante cafés par ici, un à deux minutes d'ici.

Your score: _______ %

Week 3: Test your progress

1 Vous avez vu un vendeur?
2 À quelle heure devez-vous aller en ville aujourd'hui?
3 Qui a vu Pierre hier à la télé?
4 Je crois que les magasins sont ouverts maintenant.
5 Il y a un grand magasin par ici ou au centre?
6 Excusez-moi, je dois aller à la poste. Vous aussi?
7 Où avez-vous acheté le journal anglais?
8 Le temps est mauvais aujourd'hui. Il fait froid.
9 Quoi? C'est tout? C'était très bon marché!
10 Un timbre pour l'Angleterre – c'est combien?
11 J'ai une carte de crédit: Il y a un distributeur?
12 Nous devons aller au pressing. C'est bien, pas de problème.
13 Vous avez un sac pour mes chaussures noires, s'il vous plaît?
14 Je crois que j'ai vu une pharmacie par ici.
15 Taille douze anglaise – c'est quoi en France?
16 Vous avez travaillé jusqu'à cinq heures ou plus tard?
17 Je suis désolé, nous avons mangé tout le jambon.
18 D'abord, je dois réparer le sac, et ensuite nous pouvons faire les courses.
19 Nous avons tout pris: de la bière, du vin et du fromage.
20 C'était un vendeur très sympathique.

Your score: _______ %

Week 4: Test your progress

1 Bien sûr, le rendez-vous était mercredi à la banque.
2 La semaine prochaine? Non, ce n'est pas possible. Nous n'avons pas le temps.
3 Je voudrais un verre de champagne et ensuite une bouteille de vin blanc.

4 Pouvez-vous m'aider, s'il vous plaît. Quelqu'un a besoin du numéro du médecin.
5 Il a dit que le centre ville est très intéressant. Vous l'avez vu?
6 Nous voudrions manger avec vous lundi soir.
7 Où peut-on acheter des fruits et des légumes par ici?
8 Le distributeur est en haut, devant la sortie.
9 Nous prenons le poulet ou la salade au jambon. Le poisson est trop cher.
10 Je connais bien les vins de Bordeaux. Ils sont superbes.
11 Vendredi, nous allons chez le client. C'est une affaire très importante.
12 Je voudrais acheter quelque chose. Comment dit-on en français...?
13 Je n'aime pas la Mercédès. Je vais prendre la petite Peugeot.
14 Il dit qu'il a la grippe et qu'il n'a pas terminé le travail.
15 Tout le monde a téléphoné ce soir. C'est fou!
16 Qui a vu que le chien a mangé ma viande?
17 Il y a de la glace. Mais je n'aime pas la glace au chocolat.
18 Ça va? Vous êtes malade? Vous devez boire beaucoup d'eau.
19 Quand allons-nous à Lyon et pourquoi?
20 Que faisons-nous dans cet hôtel? C'est horrible.

Your score: ______ %

Week 5: Test your progress

1 À quelle heure est le prochain bus?
2 C'est combien un aller-retour?
3 Qu'est-ce que vous avez dit? Pouvez-vous parler plus lentement s'il vous plaît?
4 Je ne comprends pas pourquoi l'essence est moins chère en Amérique.
5 C'est interdit de fumer dans le métro.
6 Vite, voilà le train. Quai trois.
7 Cette boîte est pour les cartes postales? Une boîte jaune?
8 Allô, je viens de Calais. C'est le garage?
9 J'espère que ce n'est pas la dernière station-service.
10 Il fait très chaud cette semaine. Je voudrais un peu de pluie.
11 Elle n'a pas attendu le feu rouge. Maintenant elle est à l'hôpital.
12 Nous n'avons pas vu beaucoup de soleil. Je ne suis pas content.
13 Elle parle et fume trop sur l'autoroute! Je vais prendre le train.
14 Nous sommes à la police parce que quelqu'un a pris notre téléphone portable.

15 Les billets sont bon marché si vous les achetez maintenant.
16 J'aime votre Ferrari. Elle était très chère?
17 Il y a une pharmacie derrière la rue principale, à côté de l'arrêt du bus.
18 Comment est la voiture? Elle est vieille mais le moteur est nouveau.
19 J'ai besoin de deux billets. Il y a des places non-fumeurs?
20 Excusez-moi, je ne connais pas la ville. Où est la gare?

Your score: _______ %

Week 6: Test your progress

1 Nous écrivons beaucoup de courriers électroniques/e-mails parce que nous avons un ordinateur.
2 Ça va? Qu'est-ce qu'il y a? Je peux vous aider?
3 Nous venons avec beaucoup de gens du bureau.
4 Il a dit que nous allons dîner avec des amis.
5 Pendant les vacances de Noël il y a toujours beaucoup de neige.
6 La deuxième valise est dans le bus. Pouvez-vous prendre le sac noir?
7 C'est fou. Je crois que quelqu'un a mangé mon steak!
8 Pourquoi vous n'avez pas téléphoné? Nous avons attendu jusqu'à hier.
9 Vite! Avez-vous vu un taxi? Mon avion attend.
10 Je le sais. L'aéroport est toujours ouvert – jour et nuit.
11 J'ai travaillé sur un bateau mais le travail n'était pas bien payé.
12 Je voudrais dîner plus tard. À huit heures et demie. Ça va?
13 Votre mère est très sympathique et elle fait des gâteaux merveilleux.
14 Vous avez pris un appartement à Londres ou sur la côte?
15 Nous devons travailler beaucoup d'heures. Trois garçons et deux filles à l'école – c'est trop d'argent.
16 J'espère que le garage peut le réparer.
17 Je la connais. Elle fait toujours les courses avec son chien.
18 Qui a dit qu'il est interdit de fumer par ici?
19 Je voudrais parler avec le vendeur, s'il vous plaît. Il m'a donné des chaussures vertes!
20 Ils disent que vous avez acheté une autre Citroën.
21 Qu'est-ce que vous voudriez boire? Nous avons un vin rouge superbe.
22 Dimanche et lundi le bateau part à six heures moins le quart.
23 Je suis désolé(e), mais **Traveller's French** est terminé.

Your score: _______ %

Week 6: Say it simply

1 Excusez-moi, j'ai un problème. Ici/ça, je ne sais pas ce que c'est. Peut-être du vin rouge, peut-être autre chose. Mais nous partons demain. C'est possible de le faire pour ce soir, s'il vous plaît?

2 Bonjour. Mon nom est... Kate Walker. J'étais dans la chambre douze jusqu'à aujourd'hui. J'ai des choses dans la chambre mais je suis maintenant à l'aéroport. J'ai besoin de mes choses à Birmingham mais j'ai un avion à prendre. Pouvez-vous m'aider, s'il vous plaît? Puis-je vous donner mon adresse? C'est... Merci bien.

Week 6: Spot the keys

1 It depends when you are going. Normally it takes 20 minutes. But if there is a lot of traffic and the bridge is clogged up, it takes three quarters of an hour. The price is registered on the meter. Normally it is about 40, 50 euros.

2 They had of course been in... England!

French–English dictionary

In this section you'll find all the **New words** that you have learned, including the 'extras', in alphabetical order.

To make it easy for you to find what you may have forgotten, words are shown exactly as they appear in the **New words** section. For example, if you learned *a few* you'll find it under 'a'. If you don't remember how to say *I work* you'll find it under 'I'.

The only exceptions to this are the nouns. We've put the article, e.g *the* or **un**, following the noun. So you'll find *the money* under 'm' and **un jour** under 'j'.

a has
à to, at
à ... heure(s) at ... o'clock
à côté de next to, at the side of
à droite on the right
à gauche on the left
à la neige in the snow
à ma taille in my size
à Noël at Christmas
à quelle heure? at what time?
acheter to buy
actuellement now, at present
addition, l' the bill
adorable adorable, gorgeous
aéroport, l' the airport
affaire, une a matter
aidé helped
aider to help
aller to go
aller-retour return ticket (*lit.* go-return)
aller simple one way (ticket)
allô hello! *(on the telephone)*
alors so, then, now then, well
américain(e) American
amie, une a girlfriend
an, un a year
anglais(e) English
Angleterre England
année, l' the *(course of the)* year
ans, les the years
août August
appartement, l' the apartment
après afterwards, later

argent, d' of money
argent, l' the money
arrêt (de bus), l' the (bus) stop
assez (de) enough (of)
attendez! wait!
attendre to wait
attendu waited
au lait with milk
au revoir goodbye
aujourd'hui today
aussi also, too
autoroute, l' the motorway
autre other
avec with
avez-vous? do you have? *(polite)*
avion, l' the aeroplane
avril april

bain, le the bath
banque, la the bank
bateau, un a boat
beau beautiful
beaucoup (de) much, a lot (of)
belle beautiful
beurre, le the butter
bien well
bien payé well paid
bien sûr sure, of course
bière, la the beer
billet, le the ticket
blanc, blanche white
bleu, bleue blue
boire to drink
boîte, la the box
bon marché cheap
bon, bonne good
bonjour good day, good morning, good afternoon, hello
bonne nuit good night
bonsoir good evening
bout, le the end
bouteille, la the bottle
brun, brune brown
bureau, le the office
bus, le the bus

c'est it is, this is
c'est bien that's all right
Ça coûte cher. It costs a lot.
Ça va? How are you?
café, le the coffee, the café
café crème, le the white coffee
carte, la the map
carte de crédit, la the credit card
carte postale, la the postcard
ce this
ce matin this morning
ce soir this evening
celle-ci this one
celui-ci this one
cent hundred
centime, le the cent *(part of euro)*
centre ville, le the town centre
cette this
chambre, la the room
chaud(e) hot
chaussures, les the shoes

chez at
chez des amis at/to friends
chien, un a dog
choses, les the things
cinq five
cinquante fifty
client, un a client
coiffeur, le the hairdresser
combien? how much, how many?
comme like, *also:* how
comment how, what, pardon?
comment dit-on? how does one say?
content(e) pleased
côte, la the coast
couleurs, les the colours
courriel, le e-mail
crème (fraîche), la the cream

d'abord first
d'accord all right, agreed
dans in, inside
de of, from
de … à from … to
décembre December
demain tomorrow
demi kilo, un half a kilo
dernier, le the last
dernière, la the last
derrière behind
dessert du jour, le the dessert of the day
deux two
deuxième, le/la the second
devant in front of
difficile difficult
dimanche Sunday
dîné eaten out, dined
dîner to eat out, dine
distributeur (automatique), le the cashpoint machine
dix ten
dix-huit (ten-eight) eighteen
dix-neuf (ten-nine) nineteen
dix-sept (ten-seven) seventeen
donné given
donner to give
douche, la the shower
douze twelve

école, l' the school
église, l' the church
elle she, it
elle donne she gives
en in, at
en bas down below
en français in French
en haut above, upstairs
en panne broken down, not working
en plastique plastic
en route on the move
enfants, les the children
ensuite then, next, finally
essence, l' the petrol
est is
est-ce que…? is it that…? *(used to start a question)*
et and
et demie and half, half past
et quart and quarter, quarter past

exactement exactly
excusez-moi excuse me

faire to do, make
faire les courses to do the shopping
femme, la the wife, woman
feu rouge, le the traffic light
février February
fille, la the girl
folle mad, crazy
fou mad, crazy
froid(e) cold
fromage, le the cheese
fruits, les the fruit
fumé smoked
fumer to smoke

Galeries Lafayette chain of department stores
garage, le the garage, workshop
garçon, le the boy
gare, la the railway station
gâteau, le the cake
gâteaux, les the cakes
gens, les the people
glace, la the ice cream
grand(e) big
grand magasin, le the department store
grippe, la flu
gris, grise grey

heure, l' the time, hour
heure, une an hour
hier yesterday
hôpital, l' the hospital
horrible horrible
huile, l' the oil
huit eight

ici here
il a dit he has said/said
il a téléphoné he has telephoned
il dit he says
il était he was
il fait froid it is (*lit*. makes) cold
il fume he smokes
il part he, it leaves
il peut he can
il sait he knows *(a fact)*
il y a there is, there are
ils attendent/attendu they wait/waited
ils disent/dit they say/said
ils étaient they were
ils téléphonent they phone
important(e) important
interdit forbidden
intéressant(e) interesting

j'ai I have
j'ai acheté I have bought, I bought
j'ai besoin de I have need of, I need
j'ai vu I have seen, I saw
j'aime I like, love
j'espère/espéré I hope/hoped
j'étais I was
jamais never, ever

jambon, le the ham
janvier January
jaune yellow
je I
je connais/connu I know/ known *(a person or place)*
je crois I believe
je dois I must
je ne comprends pas I do not understand
je peux I can
je sais I know *(a fact)*
je suis I am
je suis désolé(e) I am sorry
je travaille I work
je vais I go, I am going
je viens I come
je vois/vu I see/seen
jeudi Thursday
jour, un a day
journal, le the newspaper
jours de la semaine, les the days of the week
juillet July
juin June
jusqu'à until

l' the
la the
la (on its own) her, it
là-bas over there
le the
le (on its own) him, it
légumes, les the vegetables
lente slow
lentement slowly
les the
lettre, la the letter
leur them
litre, le the litre
livre, le the book
lui him
lundi Monday

ma my
Madame Mrs
magasin, le the shop
mai May
maintenant now
mais but
maison, une a house
malade ill, sick
malheureuse-ment unfortunately
manger to eat
mardi Tuesday
mari, le the husband
marron brown
mars March
mauvais(e) bad
maux de tête, les the headaches
médecin, le the doctor
même … que, le/la the same … as
menu, le the menu
merci thank you
merci beaucoup thank you very much
merci bien thank you very much
mercredi Wednesday
mère, la the mother
merveilleux (-euse) wonderful
mes my

métro, le the metro (underground)
mieux better
minute, la/une the/a minute
moi me
moins less
moins le quart *lit*. less the quarter, quarter to
mois, un a month
moment, un a/one moment
mon my
Mon Dieu! My God!
moteur, le the engine
mousse au chocolat, la the chocolate mousse

ne ... pas not
neuf nine
neuf heures nine hours, nine o'clock
noir, noire black
nom, le the name
non no
non-fumeur non-smoking
notre our
nous we
nous allons we go, we are going
nous avons we have
nous avons le temps we have time
nous avons mangé we have eaten, we ate
nous connaissons we know
nous devons we must
nous écrivons/avons écrit we write/written
nous étions we were
nous faisons/avons fait we do, make/done, made
nous pouvons we can
nous prenons we take
nous sommes we are
nous venons we come, are coming
nous voudrions we would like
nouveau new
nouvelle new
novembre November
nuit, la the night
numéro(s), le(s) the number(s)

octobre October
oeufs, les the eggs
on one (*as in:* one should not ...)
onze eleven
orange orange
ordinateurs, (des) computers
ou or
où? where?
oui yes
ouvert(e) open

pain, le the bread
papier, le the paper
par ici around here
parce que because
parlé spoken
parler to speak
partir to leave
(ne) ... pas no, not
pas de no, not

pas de problème no problem
pas mal not bad
pendant during
personne nobody
petit(e) small
petit déjeuner, le the breakfast
peut-être perhaps, *lit.* can be
pharmacie, la the chemist's
photo, la the photo
places, les the seats
plein(e) full
pluie, la the rain
plus more
plus tard later
poisson, un a fish
police, la the police
pommes de terre, les the potatoes
(téléphone) portable, le the mobile (phone)
porte, la the door
possible possible
poste, la the post office
poste, un a post, position, job
potage, un a soup
poulet grillé, le the grilled chicken
pour for
pourquoi why
premier, le the first
première, la first, the
prendre to take
pressing, le the dry cleaner's
prix, le the price
prochain(e) next
propre clean
puis-je? can I?

qu'est-ce qu'il y a? what is there?/what is the matter?
qu'est-ce que ...? what? *lit.* what is it that ...?
quai, le the platform
quand when
quarante forty
quarante-sept forty-seven
quatorze fourteen
quatre four
quatre-vingt-dix (4 x 20 + 10) ninety
quatre-vingts (4 x 20) eighty
que what
que faites-vous? what do you do?
quelqu'un someone
quelque chose something
quelques jours a few days
question, la the question
qui who
quinze fifteen
quoi what

rendez-vous, le the meeting
réparer to repair
rien nothing
rose pink
rouge red
rue principale, la the main road

s'il vous plaît please
sac, le the bag

salade, la the salad
salut hi
samedi Saturday
sans without
seize sixteen
semaine, la/une the/a week
sept seven
septembre September
serveur, le the waiter
ses parents his/her parents
seulement only
si if, so
six six
snob snob, snobbish
soixante sixty
soixante et onze (60 + 11) seventy-one
soixante-dix (60 + 10) seventy
soleil, le the sun
sont are
sortie, la the exit
souvent often
station, la metro stop, station (bus)
station-service, la the petrol station
sucre, le the sugar
superbe super, superb
supermarché, le the supermarket
sur on
sympathique nice, pleasant

table, la the table
télé(vision), la the TV
téléphone, au on the telephone
téléphone, le the telephone
temps, le the weather
terminé(e) finished
thé, le the tea
timbres, les the stamps
toilettes, les the toilets
toujours always
tout(e) all
tout droit straight ahead
tout le monde everyone
train, le the train
travail, le the work
treize thirteen
trente thirty
très very
trois three
trop too
trop de … too much, too many …

un one, a
un peu a little
une a

vacances, les the holidays
vendeur, le the sales assistant
vendredi Friday
venir to come
verre d'eau, un a glass of water
vert, verte green
viande, une a meat
vieille old
vieux old
ville, une a town
vin, le the wine
vingt twenty

vingt et un twenty-one
vingt-deux twenty-two
vingt-trois twenty-three
vite quick, quickly
voici here is
voilà here is, there is
voiture, la the car
vous you *(polite)*
vous désirez you would like
vous êtes you are *(polite)*
vous pouvez m'aider? can you help me?

zéro zero

English–French dictionary

a **un, une**
a few days **quelques jours**
a little **un peu**
a lot (of) **beaucoup (de)**
above **en haut**
adorable **adorable**
aeroplane, the **l'avion**
afterwards **après**
agreed **d'accord**
airport, the **l'aéroport**
all **tout(e)**
all right **d'accord**
also **aussi**
always **toujours**
American **américain(e)**
and **et**
apartment, the **l'appartement**
April **avril**
are **sont**
around here **par ici**
at **à, chez, en**
at ... o'clock **à ... heure/s**
at present **actuellement**
at the side of **à côté de**
at what time? **à quelle heure?**
August **août**

bad **mauvais(e)**
bag, the **le sac**
bank, the **la banque**
bath, the **le bain**
beautiful **beau, belle**
because **parce que**
beer, the **la bière**
behind **derrière**
better **mieux**
big **grand(e)**
bill, the **l'addition**
black **noir, noire**
blue **bleu, bleue**
boat, a **un bateau**
book, the **le livre**
bottle, the **la bouteille**
box, the **la boîte**
boy, the **le garçon**
bread, the **le pain**
breakfast, the **le petit déjeuner**
broken down **en panne**
brown **brun, brune, marron**
bus, the **le bus**
bus stop, the **l'arrêt (de bus)**
but **mais**
butter, the **le beurre**
buy (to) **acheter**

café, the **le café**
cake/cakes, the **le gâteau/ les gâteaux**
can I? **puis-je?**

can you help me? **vous pouvez m'aider?**
car, the **la voiture**
cashpoint machine, the **le distributeur (automatique)**
cent *(part of euro)*, the **le centime**
chain of department stores **Galeries Lafayette**
cheap **bon marché**
cheese, the **le fromage**
chemist's, the **la pharmacie**
children, the **les enfants**
chocolate mousse, the **la mousse au chocolat**
Christmas, at Christmas **Noël, à Noël**
church, the **l'église**
clean **propre**
client, a **un client**
coast, the **la côte**
coffee, the **le café**
cold **froid(e)**
colours, the **les couleurs**
come (to) **venir**
computers **(des) ordinateurs**
crazy **fou/folle**
cream, the **la crème (fraîche)**
credit card, the **la carte de crédit**

day, a **un jour**
days of the week, the **les jours de la semaine**
December **décembre**
department store, the **le grand magasin**
dessert of the day, the **le dessert du jour**
difficult **difficile**
dine (to) **dîner**
dined **dîné**
do (to) **faire**
do the shopping (to) **faire les courses**
do you have? *(polite)* **avez-vous?**
doctor, the **le médecin**
dog, a **un chien**
door, the **la porte**
down below **en bas**
drink (to) **boire**
dry cleaner's, the **le pressing**
during **pendant**

eat (to) **manger**
eat out (to) **dîner**
eaten out **dîné**
eggs, the **les oeufs**
eight **huit**
eighteen **dix-huit** (ten-eight)
eighty **quatre-vingts** (4 x 20)
eleven **onze**
e-mail **le courriel**
end, the **le bout**
engine, the **le moteur**
England **Angleterre**
English **anglais(e)**
enough (of) **assez (de)**
ever **jamais**
everyone **tout le monde**
exactly **exactement**

excuse me **excusez-moi**
exit, the **la sortie**

February **février**
fifteen **quinze**
fifty **cinquante**
finally **ensuite**
finished **terminé(e)**
first **d'abord**
first, the **le premier/ la première**
fish, a **un poisson**
five **cinq**
flu **la grippe**
for **pour**
forbidden **interdit**
forty **quarante**
forty-seven **quarante-sept**
four **quatre**
fourteen **quatorze**
French **français**
French, in **français, en**
Friday **vendredi**
friends, at/to friends **des amis, chez des amis**
from **de**
from … to **de … à**
fruit, the **les fruits**
full **plein(e)**

garage, the **le garage**
girl, the **la fille**
girlfriend, a **une amie**
give (to) **donner**
given **donné**
glass of water, a **un verre d'eau**
go (to) **aller**
good **bon, bonne**
good afternoon **bonjour**
good day **bonjour**
good evening **bonsoir**
good morning **bonjour**
good night **bonne nuit**
goodbye **au revoir**
gorgeous **adorable**
green **vert, verte**
grey **gris, grise**
grilled chicken, the **le poulet grillé**

hairdresser, the **le coiffeur**
half a kilo **un demi kilo**
half past **et demie**
ham, the **le jambon**
has **a**
he can **il peut**
he has said/said **il a dit**
he has telephoned **il a téléphoné**
he knows *(a fact)* **il sait**
he, it leaves **il part**
he says **il dit**
he smokes **il fume**
he was **il était**
headache(s), the **les maux de tête**
hello **bonjour**
hello! *(on the telephone)* **allô**
help (to) **aider**
helped **aidé**
her, it **la** (on its own)
here **ici**
here is **voici, voilà**
hi **salut**

him **lui**
him, it **le** (on its own)
holidays, the **les vacances**
horrible **horrible**
hospital, the **l'hôpital**
hot **chaud(e)**
hour, an/the **une/l'heure**
house, a **une maison**
how? **comment?**
how are you? **ça va?**
how does one say ... ? **comment dit-on ... ?**
how many? **combien?**
how much? **combien?**
hundred **cent**
husband, the **le mari**

I **je**
I am **je suis**
I am going **je vais**
I am sorry **je suis désolé(e)**
I believe **je crois**
I can **je peux**
I come **je viens**
I do not understand **je ne comprends pas**
I go **je vais**
I have **j'ai**
I have bought, I bought **j'ai acheté**
I have seen, I saw **j'ai vu**
I hope/hoped **j'espère/espéré**
I know *(a fact)* **je sais**
I know/known *(a person or place)* **je connais/connu**
I like, love **j'aime**
I must **je dois**
I need, I have need of **j'ai besoin de**
I see **je vois**
I was **j'étais**
I work **je travaille**
ice cream, the **la glace**
if **si**
ill **malade**
important **important(e)**
in **en, dans**
in front of **devant**
inside **dans**
interesting **intéressant(e)**
is **est**
is it that ... ? *(used to start a question)* **est-ce que ... ?**
it costs a lot **ça coûte cher**
it is **c'est**
it is (*lit.* makes) cold **il fait froid**

January **janvier**
job, a **un poste**
July **juillet**
June **juin**

last, the **le dernier/la dernière**
later **après, plus tard**
leave (to) **partir**
less **moins**
letter, the **la lettre**
like **comme**
litre, the **le litre**

mad **fou/folle**
main road, the **la rue principale**

make (to) **faire**
map, the **la carte**
March **mars**
matter, a **une affaire**
May **mai**
me **moi**
meat, the **la viande**
meeting, the **le rendez-vous**
menu, the **le menu**
metro (under-ground), the **le métro**
metro stop **la station**
minute, a **une minute**
mobile (phone), the **le (téléphone) portable**
moment, a/one **un moment**
Monday **lundi**
money, of money **d'argent**
money, the **l'argent**
months, the **les mois**
more **plus**
mother, the **la mère**
motorway, the **l'autoroute**
Mrs **Madame**
much **beaucoup (de)**
my **mon, ma, mes**
my God! **mon Dieu!**

name, the **le nom**
never **jamais**
new **nouveau, nouvelle**
newspaper, the **le journal**
next **prochain(e), ensuite**
next to **à côté de**
nice **sympathique**
night, the **la nuit**
nine **neuf**
nine hours, nine o'clock **neuf heures**
nineteen **dix-neuf** (ten-nine)
ninety **quatre-vingt-dix** (4 x 20 + 10)
no **non**
no, not **(ne) ... pas, pas de**
no problem **pas de problème**
nobody **personne**
non-smoking **non-fumeur**
not bad **pas mal**
not working **en panne**
nothing **rien**
November **novembre**
now **actuellement, maintenant**
now then **alors**
number, the **le numéro**

October **octobre**
of **de**
of course **bien sûr**
office, the **le bureau**
often **souvent**
oil, the **l'huile**
old **vieux, vieille**
on **sur**
on the left **à gauche**
on the move **en route**
on the right **à droite**
on the telephone **au téléphone**
one **un**
one (*as in:* one should ...) **on**
one way (ticket) **aller simple**
only **seulement**
open **ouvert(e)**

or **ou**
orange **orange**
other **autre**
our **notre**
over there **là-bas**

paper, the **le papier**
pardon? **comment?**
parents, his/her parents **des parents, ses parents**
people, the **les gens**
perhaps, *lit.* can be **peut-être**
petrol station, the **la station-service**
petrol, the **l'essence**
photo, the **la photo**
pink **rose**
plastic **en plastique**
platform, the **le quai**
pleasant **sympathique**
please **s'il vous plaît**
pleased **content(e)**
police, the **la police**
position, a **un poste**
possible **possible**
post, a (job) **un poste**
post office, the **la poste**
postcard, the **la carte postale**
potatoes, the **les pommes de terre**
price, the **le prix**

quarter past **et quart**
quarter to, *lit.* less the quarter **moins le quart**
question, the **la question**
quick, quickly **vite**

railway station, the **la gare**
rain, the **la pluie**
red **rouge**
repair (to) **réparer**
return ticket, *lit.* go-return **aller-retour**
room, the **la chambre**

salad, the **la salade**
sales assistant, the *(male)* **le vendeur**
same … as, the **le/la même … que,**
Saturday **samedi**
school, the **l'école**
seats, the **les places**
second, the **le/la deuxième**
September **septembre**
seven **sept**
seventeen **dix-sept** (ten-seven)
seventy **soixante-dix** (60 + 10)
seventy-one **soixante et onze** (60 + 11)
she gives **elle donne**
she, it **elle**
shoes, the **les chaussures**
shop, the **le magasin**
shower, the **la douche**
sick **malade**
six **six**
sixteen **seize**
sixty **soixante**
size, in my size **taille, à ma taille**
slow **lente**

slowly **lentement**
small **petit(e)**
smoke (to) **fumer**
smoked **fumé**
snob, snobbish **snob**
snow, in the snow **neige, à la neige**
so **si, alors**
someone **quelqu'un**
something **quelque chose**
soup, a **un potage**
speak (to) **parler**
spoken **parlé**
stamps, the **les timbres**
station (bus), the **la station**
straight ahead **tout droit**
sugar, the **le sucre**
sun, the **le soleil**
Sunday **dimanche**
super, superb **superbe**
supermarket, the **le supermarché**
sure **bien sûr**

table, the **la table**
take (to) **prendre**
tea, the **le thé**
telephone, the **le téléphone**
ten **dix**
thank you **merci**
thank you very much **merci beau coup, merci bien**
that's all right **c'est bien**
the **l', le, la, les**
them **leur**
then **alors, ensuite**
there are **il y a**
there is **voilà, il y a**
they phone **ils téléphonent**
they say/said **ils disent/dit**
they wait/waited **ils attendent/attendu**
they were **ils étaient**
things, the **choses, les**
thirteen **treize**
thirty **trente**
this **ce, cette**
this evening **ce soir**
this is **c'est**
this morning **ce matin**
this one **celui-ci, celle-ci**
three **trois**
Thursday **jeudi**
ticket, the **le billet**
time, the **l'heure**
to **à**
today **aujourd'hui**
toilets, the **les toilettes**
tomorrow **demain**
too **aussi, trop**
too many .../too much **trop de ...**
town centre, the **le centre ville**
town, a **une ville**
traffic light, the **le feu rouge**
train, the **le train**
Tuesday **mardi**
TV, the **la télé(vision)**
twelve **douze**
twenty **vingt**
twenty-one **vingt et un**
twenty-three **vingt-trois**
twenty-two **vingt-deux**
two **deux**

unfortunately **malheureusement**
until **jusqu'à**
upstairs **en haut**

vegetables, the **les légumes**
very **très**

wait! **attendez!**
wait (to) **attendre**
waited **attendu**
waiter, the **le serveur**
we **nous**
we are **nous sommes**
we can **nous pouvons**
we come, are coming **nous venons**
we do/done **nous faisons/ fait**
we go, we are going **nous allons**
we have **nous avons**
we have eaten, we ate **nous avons mangé**
we have time **nous avons le temps**
we know **nous connais-sons**
we make/made **nous faisons/fait**
we must **nous devons**
we take **nous prenons**
we were **nous étions**
we would like **nous voudrions**
we write/written **nous écrivons/écrit**
weather, the **le temps**
Wednesday **mercredi**
week, a/the **une/la semaine**
well **alors, bien**
well paid **bien payé**
what **que, quoi**
what? **comment?**
what? (*lit.* what is it that…?) **qu'est-ce que…?**
what do you do? **que faites-vous?**
what is there?/what is the matter? **qu'est-ce qu'il y a?**
when **quand**
where? **où?**
white **blanc, blanche**
white coffee, the **le café crème**
who **qui**
why **pourquoi**
wife, the **la femme**
wine, the **le vin**
with **avec**
with milk **au lait**
without **sans**
woman, the **la femme**
wonderful **merveilleux (-euse)**
work, the **le travail**
workshop, the **le garage**

year, a/the **un/l'an**
year, the *(course of the year)* **l'année**
yellow **jaune**
yes **oui**
yesterday **hier**
you *(polite)* **vous**
you are *(polite)* **vous êtes**
you would like **vous désirez**

How to use the flash cards

Learning words and sentences can be tedious but with flash cards it's quick and good fun.

This is what you do

When the **Day-by-day guide** tells you to use the cards cut them out, photocopy them or copy them on to card. There are 22 **Flash words** and 10 **Flash sentences** for each week. Each card has a little number on it telling you to which week it belongs, so you won't cut out too many cards at a time or muddle them up later on.

First try to learn the words and sentences by looking at both sides. Then, when you have a rough idea, start testing yourself – that's the fun bit. Look at the English, say the French and then check. Make a pile for 'correct' and one for 'wrong' and 'don't know'. When all the cards are used up, start again with the 'wrong' pile and try to whittle it down until you have got all of them right. You can also play it 'backwards' by starting with the French face-up.

Take them with you on the bus, the train, to the hairdresser's or the dentist. Do a quick 'turn and learn' whenever you have a bit of spare time.

The 22 **Flash words** of each lesson are there to start you off. Convert the rest of the **New words** to **Flash cards**, too.

Flash cards for fast learning: **Don't lose them – use them!**

1 excusez-moi	1 s'il vous plaît
1 malheureuse-ment	1 aussi
1 mais	1 dans
1 très	1 beau, belle
1 pour	1 le travail
1 que	1 chez

Cut out and use ✂

1 please	1 excuse me
1 also	1 unfortunately
1 in	1 but
1 beautiful	1 very
1 the work	1 for
1 at, to (someone)	1 what, *also:* that

Cut out and use

1 **ne ... pas**	1 **mieux**
1 **cher, chère**	1 **je**
1 **nous**	1 **vous**
1 **avec**	1 **j'ai besoin de**
1 **l'argent**	1 **avez-vous?**
2 **en panne**	2 **peut-être**

Cut out and use

1 **better**	1 **not**
1 **I**	1 **expensive**
1 **you**	1 **we**
1 **I need**	1 **with**
1 **do you have?**	1 **the money**
2 **perhaps**	2 **broken**

Cut out and use

2 réparer	2 où
2 ici	2 à gauche
2 assez	2 combien?
2 seulement	2 il y a
2 d'accord	2 demain
2 autre	2 à droite

Cut out and use

2

where

2

to repair

2

on the left

2

here

2

how much,
how many?

2

enough

2

there is,
there are

2

only

2

tomorrow

2

agreed,
all right

2

on the right

2

other

Cut out and use

2 **ensuite**	2 **quelque chose**
2 **trop**	2 **un peu**
2 **moins**	2 **le mari**
2 **il peut**	2 **les toilettes**
3 **aujourd'hui**	3 **timbres**
3 **tout(e)**	3 **d'abord**

Cut out and use

2 something	2 next, then
2 a little	2 too much, too many
2 the husband	2 less
2 the toilets	2 he can
3 stamps	3 today
3 first	3 all

Cut out and use

3 **après**	3 **Mon Dieu!**
3 **jusqu'à**	3 **ouvert(e)**
3 **je dois**	3 **plus tard**
3 **un distributeur (de banque)**	3 **le pain**
3 **une bouteille**	3 **comme**
3 **qui**	3 **quoi**

Cut out and use

3 **My God!**	3 **after, afterwards**
3 **open**	3 **until**
3 **later**	3 **I must**
3 **the bread**	3 **a cashpoint machine**
3 **like, as**	3 **a bottle**
3 **what**	3 **who**

Cut out and use

3 **le magasin**	3 **hier**
3 **la pharmacie**	3 **le beurre**
3 **je crois**	3 **mauvais**
4 **boire**	4 **quand**
4 **bien sûr**	4 **derrière**
4 **en haut**	4 **je connais**

Cut out and use

3 yesterday	3 the shop
3 the butter	3 the pharmacy
3 bad	3 I believe
4 when	4 to drink
4 behind	4 sure, of course
4 I know	4 above, upstairs

Cut out and use

4 je peux/ puis-je?	4 la glace
4 la sortie	4 rien
4 malade	4 personne
4 pourquoi	4 quelqu'un
4 prochain(e)	4 devant
4 l'église	4 un poisson

Cut out and use

4 the ice cream	4 I can/can I?
4 nothing	4 the exit
4 nobody	4 sick, ill
4 someone	4 why
4 in front of	4 next
4 a fish	4 the church

Cut out and use

4 **la grippe**	4 **les légumes**
4 **un chien**	4 **les maux**
5 **la gare**	5 **comment?**
5 **là-bas**	5 **non-fumeur**
5 **l'arrêt**	5 **parce que**
5 **la boîte**	5 **celui-ci, celle-ci**

Cut out and use

4 the vegetables	4 the flu
4 the pains	4 a dog
5 how, what, pardon?	5 the station
5 non-smoking	5 over there
5 because	5 the stop
5 this one	5 the box

Cut out and use

5

plein(e)

5

notre

5

la voiture

5

vieux, vieille

5

la rue principale

5

l'autoroute

5

l'essence

5

le dernier, la dernière

5

j'espère

5

attendre

5

le problème

5

je comprends

Cut out and use

5 our	5 full
5 old	5 the car
5 the motorway	5 the main road
5 the last	5 the petrol
5 to wait	5 I hope
5 I understand	5 the problem

Cut out and use

5 le billet	5 content(e)
6 l'aéroport	6 partir
6 jamais	6 ils disent
6 les gens	6 leur
6 je sais	6 à Noël
6 un bateau	6 voici

Cut out and use

5 **pleased**	5 **the ticket**
6 **to leave**	6 **the airport**
6 **they say**	6 **never, ever**
6 **them**	6 **the people**
6 **at Christmas**	6 **I know**
6 **here is**	6 **a ship**

Cut out and use

6 merveilleux (-euse)	6 nous connaissons
6 venir	6 donner
6 je vois	6 souvent
6 pendant	6 l'appartement
6 le livre	6 la fille
6 la mère	6 nous écrivons

Cut out and use

6 we know	6 wonderful
6 to give	6 to come
6 often	6 I see
6 the flat, apartment	6 during
6 the girl	6 the book
6 we write	6 the mother

Cut out and use

J'étais trois ans à New York. 1

Je travaille pour la banque. 1

J'ai un bon poste. 1

Je n'ai pas une grande maison. 1

Nous avons deux enfants. 1

Nous sommes en vacances. 1

Nous allons à Bordeaux. 1

Avez-vous un téléphone? 1

Elle a une amie. 1

ça coûte cher 1

Cut out and use

I was in New York for three years. 1

I work for the bank. 1

I have a good job. 1

I don't have a big house. 1

We have two children. 1

We are on holiday. 1

We are going to Bordeaux. 1

Do you have a telephone? 1

She has a girlfriend. 1

this costs a lot 1

Cut out and use

Il y a un café par ici? 2

à huit heures et demie 2

à cinq heures et quart 2

l'addition, s'il vous plaît 2

Où sont les toilettes,
à gauche ou à droite? 2

La chambre, c'est combien? 2

À quelle heure est le
petit déjeuner? 2

D'accord, nous le prenons. 2

quelque chose à manger 2

Nous voudrions aller à … 2

Cut out and use

Is there a café around here? 2

at half past eight 2

at a quarter past five 2

the bill, please 2

Where are the toilets, on the left or on the right? 2

How much is the room? 2

At what time is breakfast? 2

All right, we'll take it. 2

something to eat 2

We would like to go to … 2

Cut out and use

Je suis désolé(e). 3

Je vais faire les courses. 3

Nous devons aller à … 3

jusqu'à quelle heure? 3

pas de problème 3

Qu'est-ce qu'il y a? 3

Qu'est-ce que c'est? 3

Les magasins sont ouverts. 3

Nous voudrions acheter un journal. 3

le bus pour le centre ville 3

I am sorry. 3

I am going shopping. 3

We must go to ... 3

until what time? 3

no problem 3

What is there/the matter? 3

What is that? 3

The shops are open. 3

We would like to buy a newspaper. 3

the bus for the town centre 3

Cut out and use

Il est très sympathique. 4

Il dit que ... 4

J'aime le vin rouge. 4

Vous pouvez m'aider, s'il vous plaît? 4

Comment dit-on ... en français? 4

Quelqu'un m'a dit que ... 4

Nous n'avons pas le temps. 4

la semaine prochaine 4

Je le connais. 4

Ce n'est pas possible. 4

Cut out and use

He is very nice. 4

He says that … 4

I like red wine. 4

Can you help me, please? 4

How do you say …
in French? 4

Someone told me that … 4

We don't have time. 4

next week 4

I know him. 4

That's not possible. 4

Cut out and use

Pouvez-vous parler plus lentement? 5

Deux aller-retours, s'il vous plaît. 5

deux places pour non-fumeurs 5

Je ne comprends pas. 5

Où y a-t-il une station-service? 5

Je crois que la voiture est en panne. 5

Il n'est pas cher parce qu'il est vieux. 5

Ce bus va jusqu'à la gare? 5

À quelle heure part le train? 5

Nous venons d'Angleterre. 5

Can you speak more slowly? 5

Two return tickets, please. 5

two non-smoking seats 5

I don’t understand. 5

Where is there a petrol station? 5

I think the car has broken down. 5

It is not expensive because it is old. 5

This bus goes to the station? 5

At what time does the train leave? 5

We are coming from England. 5

Cut out and use

Je ne peux pas attendre. 6

Pouvez-vous venir? 6

Il leur a donné le numéro. 6

Celui-ci est pour lui. 6

Pouvez-vous me donner …? 6

Je n'aime pas ça. 6

Qu'est-ce qu'il a dit? 6

une semaine à Noël avec moi 6

Nos vacances sont terminées. 6

Je ne l'ai pas vu. 6

Cut out and use

I cannot wait. 6

Can you come? 6

He has given them the number. 6

This one is for him. 6

Can you give me ...? 6

I do not like that. 6

What did he say? 6

a week at Christmas with me 6

Our holidays are finished. 6

I did not see him/it. 6

Cut out and use

This is to certify
that

....

has successfully completed
a six-week course of

Traveller's French

with

....

results

Date ....

Author Elizabeth Smith

Praise for Elisabeth Smith

'A language lifeline ... fun, fast and easy.'
(*The Independent*)

'The simple scripts and audio make it crystal clear ... I'm delighted with my progress.'
(*Greece* magazine)

'Its narration is laid-back and encouraging and the method is straightforward. (4-star review).'
(*Time Out*)

'The elements are simple and very straightforward ... strong encouragement ... plenty of opportunity for spoken practice. This course worked very well for me.'
(*Professional Manager* magazine)

'We think it is wonderful.'
(Tom and Maureen Peil, Preston)

'I loved the sense of humour ... Each week I did the final test with bated breath wondering if this time the little bar chart [...] would take a nose dive – but it didn't.'
(Lesly Hopkins, Twickenham)

'This isn't just a package that asks you remember the names for things in a different language this is a package that teaches ... Highly recommended.'
(Maximus)

'It really is an effective way to learn.'
(Mr R. Ellor)

'A solid product offering excellent value for money ... a great place to start.'
(A. M. Boughey)

'One of the best courses around to get you that little bit further than the basics.'
(Johannsen Krister)

more...

'The words are very clearly spoken and the form of presentation witty and lively to keep your interest, and clever choice of subject matter also keep learning interesting and aid memory. This is a very strong language course and I recommend it.'
(vh1967)

'Although I had started learning French in my 60s ... it was only when I picked up Elizabeth Smith's *Fast French* that confidence really started to come.'
(Alan Hayes)

'The Elisabeth Smith courses are a superb resource for the learner who needs to be able to speak the language in a short period of time and with a good degree of understanding.'
(Will Boyce)

'I enjoyed this book tremendously and changed my view on the whole French language.'

'This really works, and I've tried lots of French courses and always get bored, but this is great and you can actually use the words you know when you get to France – highly recommended.'
(Ms J. Plowman)

'If you are going on a short holiday or business trip to France, this is the best course you can possibly buy, without exception.'
(M. McManus)

'I was surprised at what I'd achieved after this course and recommend it.'

'This is an absolute must have ... You'll be so glad you bought it!.'
(Elodie)

Now join me on:

Facebook at www.facebook.com/elisabethsmithlanguages

Twitter at www.twitter.com/LanguagesESmith